A MOVING INQUIRY

A MOVING INQUIRY

THE ART OF PERSONAL PRACTICE

Beth Pettengill Riley &
Priscilla Stanton Auchincloss

Epigraph Books
Rhinebeck, New York

A Moving Inquiry: The Art of Personal Practice © 2019 by Beth Pettengill Riley and Priscilla Stanton Auchincloss

All rights reserved. No part of this book may be used or reproduced in any manner without written permission from the authors, except in critical articles or reviews. Please contact the authors at www.themovingwell.com.

ISBN 978-1-948796-75-0

Library of Congress control number available upon request by publisher

Cover image: *Primordial River*, by Barbara Mindell
Cover and book design by Colin Rolfe

Epigraph Books
22 East Market Street, Suite 304
Rhinebeck, NY 12572
EpigraphPS.com

A Moving Inquiry: The Art of Personal Practice is sponsored in part by Watermark Arts, an endeavor dedicated to art, education, and community-building inspired and informed by somatic movement experience.

The images and poems in this book are protected under copyright of the individual artists. The authors are grateful for permissions granted for use of the following:

Images:
Primordial River © Barbara Mindell (with the permission of Dennis Matthies)
Sand Waves © Niki Berg
Drawing © Mary Abrams
Cosmodiem, Water and Light Series © Prue Jeffries
Duck Glide © Prue Jeffries
Contrast Peace: Open Attention © Barbara Mindell (with the permission of Dennis Matthies)
Spilling Light 3 © Satya Kirsch
Conjunctio Oppositorium © Gale Marsland
Dreams and Fantasies: Orange © Niki Berg
Untitled (4 works) © Karin Lyyke Groth
Sa Nou Pa We 2.0 © Suzanne Wright Crain (at www.thecosmicbody.com)
Kathy Cassens' photographs of dancers performing "Venus" © Elaine Colandrea (p. 41 and p. 65)

Poems:
"How to Participate in Evolution" © Noelle Adamo
"The Moon" © 2016 Bobbie Ellis
"Afternoon Emergence" © 2013 Sandra Capellaro
"Two Sides" © 2014 Sandra Capellaro
"Traveler XXIX" by Antonio Machado, translation © 2019 Marcella Bottero
"Drenched in a Lake of Awareness" © 2006 Beth Pettengill Riley
"Wisteria" © 2010 Beth Pettengill Riley
"Grace" © 2017 Raine Brown
 Excerpt from "The Soil of Myself" © Raine Brown
"Love" © Claudia Catani

CONTENTS

Foreword	vii
Preface: *About Continuum*	ix
Introduction	1
Preparing for practice	5
Writing about your experience	8
WEEK 1: The Elements of Practice	11
WEEK 2: Setting Up the Experiment	17
WEEK 3: Amplifying your Practice	24
Working on the chair	30
WEEK 4: Moving Beyond the Container	33
WEEK 5: Sensation and Reflection	41
Working with pain	48
WEEK 6: A Movement Practice to Sustain You	51
Designing your own sequence	59
Essential Reading	63
Acknowledgments	64
Watermark Arts	66
About the Authors	68

FOREWORD

It is with pleasure that I introduce you to *A Moving Inquiry: The Art of Personal Practice*. My longtime Continuum colleagues Beth Pettengill Riley and Priscilla Stanton Auchincloss, both exquisite movers, teachers, and writers, as well as collaborators at Watermark Arts, have expressed in writing the essential concepts of the somatic practice originated by our mentor Emilie Conrad. With a community of Continuum practitioners around the world, Beth, Priscilla, and I have carried the seeds of Continuum in our personal practices, in our teaching, and in the ways we live our lives. This book now, too, carries those seeds.

Priscilla and Beth illuminate the artful embodiment practice of Continuum with clear, inspired writing. Going beyond concepts, they provide a container for you to directly experience and incorporate this life-affirming activity into your days. Every page of this book conveys *somatikos, the fully alive wholeness of being*, offering a template for personal growth and, dare I say, for our collective transformation.

The images and poems you find in these pages were chosen by the authors from the online galleries of Watermark Arts, featuring artworks in all media by Continuum practitioners. In a book about incorporating somatic practice into one's daily life, we found it important that the artwork come from persons whose creative expression is deeply informed by somatic experience.

The vision of Watermark Arts states that, "With awareness of the integrity of the body comes a felt experience of the interconnection of all living things." Nothing less than such felt experience of interconnection is called for now. *A Moving Inquiry* offers access to an experience of life force as precious to individual as it is to collective thriving.

At Watermark Arts we believe "…these times call on us to become generators of the culture we wish to live in." I honor Priscilla and Beth for their heartfelt, articulate contribution to this endeavor.

Perhaps you will find yourself creating art as part of your personal practice, and perhaps you will surprise yourself with a revolutionary, culture-generating idea. To quote author and poet Beth Pettengill Riley:

Slowly the deeper call
of emerging is answered by the life in the seed,
become root, become stalk,
and the urgency towards flower begins..

With the support of *A Moving Inquiry*, may you flower.

—Elaine Colandrea
Artistic Director, Watermark Arts

PREFACE

ABOUT CONTINUUM

While there are many entry points into an embodied life, for us it was the movement practice of Continuum, a body of work originated by Emilie Conrad, that provided our way in. Our backgrounds in and passion for movement have been profoundly influenced by our years of immersion in Continuum, the practice we share with you in this book. Since Emilie's death in 2014, Continuum teachers and practitioners have found ways to further her work and develop the practice of Continuum. This book is one attempt to contribute to the ongoing expression of Continuum and to preserve the seeds of life it contains.

Continuum is a radical practice—not just because it began during a radical time in human history, the 1960s, but because from its conception it was an invitation to live outside cultural norms on every level. Emilie Conrad broke through convention upon her return from living and working as a dancer and choreographer for five years in Haiti. Walking the streets of New York, where she was raised, she recognized the constraints of the culture-at-large on the body itself. A central question arose: "Can I live in my culture and not be bound by it?"

Continuum was born out of this question. The promise of Continuum lies in its affirmation of the artistry of human existence. Through movement, breath, and sound we inquire. As Continuum practitioners, we ask of our whole selves, "What can allow my life to flourish?" We ask this of our minds, hearts, relationships, collective communities, and most often we ask

NIKI BERG, *Sand Waves*

this of our organismic body: our blood, our bones, our skin, our lungs—indeed, our entire weave of living tissue that makes up what we call a body.

Our bodies are carriers of an ongoing evolutionary history whose language is the movement of water. We enter directly through wave motion and begin to nurture the vast flow of movement and information within and between our cells, our organisms as a whole, and our biosphere.

Emilie often said, "The body is context related and context created." In her book, *Life on Land,* she wrote, "The purpose of Continuum is that it is a way of restoring personal access to billions of years of intelligence that is spiraled into the very swirl of our embryonic coil."

Continuum maintains that we are part of an unfolding process that remains intact within us: "We are not separate from the awe of primary existence." Continuum provides an opportunity to recontextualize the fabric of our lives and continues to provide a flourishing of meaning, catalyzing the future we are committed to seeing for ourselves and the very future of life on Earth.

The practice offered in this book is an inquiry into human flourishing. The question is, how is one to flourish—to create the conditions to flourish as a person living in society, as a human being, as a living organism belonging to an evolutionary process? Continuum proposes a reliable set of concepts and practices to guide this inquiry at the personal level, and we are honored to share them with you here.

What could be more personal than something you do on a regular basis to nourish and inquire into the nature of your being? We think that this work has something critical to offer—a way to revive, restore, and liberate life force that is not found in other philosophical systems or somatic techniques.

Wherever your practice takes you, our hope is that you will benefit from the concepts and methods presented here. This book offers you an opportunity to dive into a movement practice with your whole heart, suspending your judgements while allowing your questions to come forward along with answers that make sense to you.

—Beth Pettengill Riley and
Priscilla Stanton Auchincloss

INTRODUCTION

Welcome to *A Moving Inquiry: The Art of Personal Practice*. You are about to embark on an exploratory journey, with your body as partner and guide. The purpose of this book is to help you establish a personal movement practice.

This book is rooted in the movement practice of Continuum, originated by Emilie Conrad in 1967. It is difficult to describe what Continuum *is* and how to do it. For most people, when hearing about Continuum, the picture in their mind conforms to some other movement modality with which they have at least a vague familiarity. For the most part, Continuum is not like any of these and in fact is so different in its very approach that the word *radical* would not be out of place.

At the heart of Continuum is the quest to restore and amplify one's life force. Emilie was able to articulate and transmit to others that summoning life force engenders a profound respect for the intelligence of the body itself. The body, being primarily fluid, has the innate capacity to move as one whole fluid system. Yet as Emilie discovered, this intrinsic fluid movement cannot be superimposed on the body—rather, only allowed to emerge

> *A meaningful practice brings positive change. Habitual tendencies preserve the status quo.*
> —Mark Nepo

as layers of conditioning are removed and certain essential skills are cultivated.

Through experience, one comes to see that the living body shares with all living systems the ability and urge to take in information—to tend to self and extend outward—to adapt, complexify, and innovate within the context of and in relationship to its environment, both natural and human-made. Within all of this—the fluid movement informing the body, a living system in communication with its greater environment, operates a kind of wordless intelligence—permeating and linking all living systems through a flow of information and interaction comprising the processes of life and existence at every level. The arising of fluid movement within the body is the expression of the stirring of this underlying flow. To practice Continuum is to grow increasingly receptive to the flow of intelligence from the natural world through one's felt senses and living tissues.

Few other practices that we have encountered nourish essential life force as directly as this one. A deeper difficulty is that so-called civilized living has alienated people from any sense of themselves as living systems, and respect for the body's intelligence may be a nice concept but rarely a way of life. Usually, in other practices the teacher tells you what to do (or you tell your body what to do). By contrast, you will find here that you are "invited" to do XYZ. There are no set moves or positions, but instead, a series of somewhat open-ended instructions. You are frequently advised to listen, pause, stop, suspend—to *attend* at ever more refined levels to the messages coming to you through subtle sensation and movement.

Nevertheless, there is a structure to this kind of practice, and there are skills to cultivate.

Continuum is considered a *somatic* movement modality. The word "somatic" refers to the felt experience of the body as one lives in it. Somatic movement practice is concerned not with performance—how the movement looks or what meaning it might be expressing to an audience—but with the person's direct sensory experience of movement.

As profound an influence as Continuum has been in shaping the mode of practice offered here, for a number of reasons we have chosen to refer only rarely to "Continuum" in the main text. As we have said, the name is quite opaque to persons without any prior experience of the work and, on the other hand, already laden with significance for many persons who have already studied and/or practiced it. We have tried to get beyond our own assumptions about Continuum, as well as assumptions about what any given reader would and would not understand in the use of that term. We wanted to seek out the essence of the work so as to help the reader in a practical way. We also wanted the freedom to present this work in terms that made sense to us.

Part of our discovery in studying and practicing Continuum has been its capacity to bring to light the qualities of living systems, as well as how to cultivate those qualities. This is a practice about all the ways one's physical biological intelligence can be made available to the enrichment of life as one participates with it. We seek to open the lens of awareness as wide as possible and focus on the tangible experience itself, rather than labeling it as a particular modality—even "Continuum."

WHAT IS "PRACTICE"?

The intent of the practice we share in this book is to bring you to a meeting with yourself – a fresh meeting, each time. It is important to understand that your felt experience is what matters here. The term we use for this is *self-referencing*. Self-referencing in this context means paying attention to your own experience as you move—to what you are doing and feeling—and becoming intimate with the range of possibilities that are arising moment by moment.

By choosing to read this book, you are *already* in the act of establishing a personal practice. What you go through in this process is part of the practice itself. You and everyone who has ever established or tried to establish a personal movement practice are contributing to what personal practice is and what this means in a human life. Your discoveries, your reasons, your ideas, your sensations, and the meaning you make of them are all at the heart of your practice.

The intent of this book is to offer a context, a kind of safe enclosure, in which to incubate your growing practice. This practice may also enlarge your understanding of what it means to you to be a human being at this time. The approach outlined here offers an investigation into felt experience not found in other practices, and it spells out certain features of practice that are often assumed but never mentioned explicitly. Throughout the book we inquire into what sustains practice and the "why" of practice. It is this kind of inquiry that leads to discovery, meaning, and a sense of fulfillment.

Ultimately, *the body is the path*. It is the way to wholeness and sense of connection to life—the way home. Practice brings an organizing and unifying consciousness to lived experience.

For a practice to be fulfilling, you have to fulfill it. There is a challenge intrinsic to practice: to keep doing it. Maintaining a practice helps you develop resilience in daily life and strengthens an internal conviction about what matters most to you. Practice fosters within you something of value that no one can take away. This is why, though it may be simple, practice is not easy.

At some point in the process of establishing and maintaining a movement practice, almost everyone needs assistance—whether through a mentor, a class structure, and/or a community of shared interest. At this time of social and ecological crisis in a world where overwhelm, anxiety, and despair are a regular occurrence for many people, the act of starting and sustaining a practice may be even more challenging, yet even more important, than ever before. In this spirit, we offer *A Moving Inquiry: The Art of Personal Practice*.

HOW TO USE THIS BOOK

This book grew out of an online course we offered in 2017, dedicated to establishing a personal movement practice in six weeks. Following that structure, the material is organized principally into six sessions, building toward a coherent movement practice. These can be done in sequence according to whatever rhythm you want.

Each session includes:
- a guided, centering *pause*;
- an introduction of the week's concepts and how they are implemented in the context of practice;
- a practice sequence introducing new breaths, movement qualities or patterns;
- a movement and journaling assignment for the coming week.

The current offering follows the basic outline of the original online course, with certain sections set apart and new material added to fill in gaps we noticed only later. The basic outline is as follows:

Guidelines for preparing your space and schedule, to signal to yourself that you are beginning something that will require space, time and attention. Your space, however modest or grand, supports your practice, providing a physical "container" as well as a helpful demarcation between everyday life and the ceremony of practice.

Guidelines for writing. At the end of each chapter you will find a short set of questions. After your practice sessions, we strongly encourage you to respond to the questions *in writing*. The intent of the written assignments is to provide "jumping off" points for your personal reflections, which could go in any number of directions.

Week 1 introduces the basic elements of *breath, sound, and movement* (what you "do"), as well as *attention* (how you engage with the elements) and *sensation* (the guide and source of information).

Week 2 lays out the arc or flow of the typical practice session, showing how to bring the elements together in a flexible yet coherent structure consistent with the interrelatedness of function and form in living systems.

Week 3 discusses ways (and why's) of expanding dynamic range—why pushing yourself out of your comfort zone is important and how it can be done while maintaining a sense of inner harmony.

Week 4 demonstrates innovation and improvisation as integral to a practice that intentionally places the body as the teacher, taking you beyond any pre-set structure and, ideally, beyond your own presumptions and stylistic habits.

Week 5 discusses the nature of sensation as a down-to-earth guide and how to engage with it authentically as vital information for working with yourself as you go through your daily life.

Week 6 looks at the sustenance offered by learning to live as a fluid body and offers ways to support your ongoing practice.

For us, *practice is an inquiry*. It is an inquiry that remains always at least somewhat open ended, without completion, finality, or full closure. Folded into the essential/universal inquiry into body/embodiment—what are we, why are we embodied—are the inquiries that have come to you in your particular life.

As an approach to the body—the attitude of inquiry, of gently asking, not ordering, demanding, or expecting it to fit a pre-known model—seems called for. That is, inquiry, while a motivation for practice, is also an attitude of practice—the attitude of nourishing one's being, bringing forth one's life force. With inquiry we remain open to the possibility that something will happen that we have not experienced and could not imagine experiencing. Something life-giving, inspiring, enlightening, uplifting. A kind of grace.

PREPARING FOR PRACTICE

*Whenever you are creating beauty around you,
you are restoring your soul.*
—Alice Walker

Preparation is everything.
—Emilie Conrad

SET UP YOUR PRACTICE SPACE

Even before you designate *time* to practice, you need an environment that supports your intent.

Between everyday time and practice time, there is an invisible line that has made practice a part of spiritual development over the ages. As you step from everyday time into practice time, it helps enormously to have a separate space, even if it is only a particular blanket that you open on the floor. The thoughts and movements that, time after time, take you into that space become a form of ceremony preparing you for what is to come. Even if your practice is not regular, you can experience a subtle shift affecting your entire being.

Beth's Practice Space

Entering your practice space, you have an opportunity to clear the slate and begin afresh. You can set aside problems in your everyday life and pick up a project or investigation you began before. What your practice space and time come to mean to you is personal, intimate, and evolving. At the same time, its designated space and time give to practice a certain formality. It is a kind of performance that is done for yourself and also for the good of all beings.

You will need:
- enough floor space to lie down and spread out;
- padding underneath (for example, a mat and blanket combination—you will learn as you go);
- other props you like to work with (such as yoga bolsters, extra blankets, weights, a chair);
- timepiece (preferably a clock or timer, not your phone);
- water, to stay hydrated;
- notebook and something to write with. Making notes on your movement experience not only strengthens your practice but also brings closure to the session, releasing you back to the rest of your life.

How much care you take in setting up your visual surroundings depends on your own sensitivities. For some it is a good practice *not* to get hung up on the aesthetics of their surroundings. For others, this is an opportunity to create a space that reflects their particular loves.

Make a schedule. To use this book as an introduction to movement practice, we suggest you go through the chapters in order, at a pace (say, weekly or every-other-week) that gives you time both to practice and to dwell with the concepts in your everyday life.

How much time should you allow each week? This choice is highly individual. A common sense suggestion is to make a plan, try it out for a couple of weeks, and then adjust. Mark down times in your week that you intend to spend in practice, totaling, say, two-and-a-half hours (or whatever duration you choose). This time would include reading the chapter, doing your movement practice, and responding in writing to the assignment. If you are drawn toward longer periods of practice or reflection, that is wonderful; if your time is more limited than you thought, adjust accordingly.

You may want to let others in your household know that you are taking time for movement/meditation practice, explaining you need to be undisturbed for that period. If it is helpful to you or them, give your reasons—health, de-stressing, rest, professional reasons—whatever. As many have found, the time taken for personal replenishment is what makes the rest of life—work, relationships, decisions, and other challenging stuff that happens—go better than it otherwise might.

PRACTICE AND JOURNALING

Assignment 1: Take a few minutes, soon, to respond to the following questions in writing. Do not delay or belabor them. Write what comes to you in the moment. Your written responses are part of the preparation process that will help you set your course toward establishing a movement practice.
- What does having a personal movement practice mean to you at this point in your life?
- What has stopped you from doing this in the past?

- What do you want from this book? How do you want your life to change by interacting with this book?

Assignment 2: Take a block of time (say, thirty to sixty minutes) to set up your space. Then, sit or lie down there. Feel how your body meets the ground. Feel the movement of your breath. Notice what sensations, images, and thoughts come to you. Stay with this inquiry for at least five minutes.

Write down some of the things you have discovered in the process of setting up your personal practice space.

Assignment 3: Look over your schedule and enter into your calendar times during the next week when you plan to engage with the material of this book. Then pause for at least five full breath cycles. Write down some of what you have experienced in the process of making a practice schedule.

WRITING ABOUT YOUR EXPERIENCE

Writing practice brings us back to the uniqueness of our own minds and an acceptance of it. We all have wild dreams, fantasies, and ordinary thoughts. Let us feel the texture of them and not be afraid of them. Writing is still the wildest thing I know.
—Natalie Goldberg, *Wild Mind: Living the Writer's Life*

MARY ABRAMS, *Drawing*

INTRODUCTION

Writing is part of developing a personal practice. In the writing process you are giving expression to some part of the experience, lifting it out of the interior realm, and giving it a place in the outer world. You are solidifying in words (spoken or written), or in artwork, some of what has taken place or is arising out of the experience.

Writing is also about making a mark in the ongoing flow of your life and evolution. After each movement session, you make notes about what you did and what you noticed in your field of sensation. You could regard this as a closing ritual for each practice session before leaving sacred space and re-entering daily life.

There are several reasons to write your reflections:

- Reflection invites you to remember what you did, what you felt, and what was new to you.
- Writing is a form of record-keeping, showing you how your practice accumulates over time and giving you a means to go back to particular sequences, insights, images, and languaging.
- By writing you give voice to your somatic experience and lift it, even imperfectly, from the ever-shifting realm of feeling and sensation to the more concrete realm of thought and language.
- Writing directly after you practice fortifies the habit and discipline of a movement practice by placing value on the realm of sensation, the language of the body. It gives a gentle but firm response to a culture that devalues the inner world.

How much you write and what you write about is up to you. Writing is simply another opportunity to engage with the process. Your responses may be long or brief. Be clear, frank, and honest with yourself.

What you reflect on will depend on what you are practicing for. This could be in preparation for teaching, for example, or fulfilling a commitment related to your health, creativity, or spiritual development.

If it is helpful to you, remember that the words are not the experience. Words are, at best, a map of the territory of experience. If you are concerned that writing and speaking are consolidating something that is meant to be fluid and whole, remember that humans create and occupy a world that is a kind of crystallization out of a greater, fluid whole. So what you write does not have to—and cannot—perfectly capture all of what you experience. Yet without writing, practice can lose the coherence that is required for living in the outer world.

In addition, bringing your experience into form, whether through spoken or written words, makes it possible to connect to other persons. Sharing your reflections with a movement partner or in a group can make your process feel more "real." Hearing others share their experiences (or read their written reflections) can further your learning by stimulating ideas and revealing new ways of relating to your own experience. Similarly, your reflections may open a door for someone else.

Yet even in a solitary home practice, the pause to reflect and write has its place. The isolation of modern life comes, perhaps most fundamentally, from not knowing how to connect to oneself. The act of writing is in itself a practice of connecting within yourself. It carries your experience from the practice period to the time just outside of practice. It prepares you to speak with inner authority when the time comes, thereby forging a bridge from within you to the outside world.

HOW TO PARTICIPATE IN EVOLUTION

First you have to hold on and remember
that you too are a part of the wind,
otherwise when you breathe
you'll feel either startled or free
and forget to listen. And then like me
you might notice the person next to you
and disconnect from the rhythm
of a hundred horses making a trail.
You'll fall into the familiar grasses
of gestures and glances and memory
or forget to move,
left in the wake of the herd.
Or you will move faster than is true,
body all jiggle and fruit and sugar lumps
with a head that nods the way
to two legs and fins and wings and none.
Your voice which always has something
new to share once again wonders
if it is brave enough to sound a singular vowel
until at last you do.
You leave nothing behind
and it tangerines the mind,
brings you to all fours so you can
slow search for the sound
that carries the tongue to the spleen
to your spine to every spine,
while the floor is nowhere
just as the field is everywhere,
and all that hums loosens you past the edge
to fingertip touch something new,
like to this vine
that was there for years to tangle you
into some form of not you, but that dies back,
then begins to sprawl with the next
sound's stretch and your attention
now to flower morning glories to yield
to the roses of the day to the moonflowers
of the night to earth wire music
from the small coos of infants
to the oceans and back
so that your palms open
and your body spreads
and you breathe
from every cell.

—Noelle Adamo

WEEK 1

THE ELEMENTS OF PRACTICE

CENTERING

Sit comfortably, and consider where you are now, at this moment, in this place. Notice what the weather systems have brought through your geographic area today. Consider the expanse of the earth with its continents, its waterways, its atmosphere. Consider how you are connected to the larger environment, even as you begin to arrive into the river of your own breath.

Now, draw your attention inward, closing your eyes if you wish. Sense into the places where your body meets the ground, and allow yourself to soften, downward, into these places.

Begin to sense the rise of the breath as you inhale, the sense of releasing and spreading as you exhale. Notice how the

PRUE JEFFRIES, *Cosmodium, Water and Light Series*

breath moves in the joints of your limbs, in the vertebrae of your spine. Gradually, focus on the movement of breath in the space of your heart.

Consider what has drawn you here at this time of your life.

Gently begin to bring your awareness back to the outer world, to the configuration of human life that happens to be with you today. Notice how the heart stays with you, the breath stays with you, the ground stays with you.

Pause for several full breath cycles, and simply notice whatever you are sensing, inwardly and outwardly.

WHAT IS A BODY?

Through the lens of modern culture, a *body* is understood predominantly as an object, a separate "thing" with particular functions. In everyday life, you take your body and carry it from place to place, or you may think of it as carrying you. Through this lens, your body is a distinct thing, among other distinct things in the world.

Living in a body is something most people take for granted, and how you relate to it can vary over time, even moment-to-moment. Under the surface of the question *what is a body?* are layers of meaning. Your body could be a source of pain or pleasure, something to "get in shape" or dress up, something valued for its strength or skill and used to get things done. Bodies have been judged and "marked" in order to confer identity and status within a social hierarchy. Most modern people feel defined and define themselves through their cultural lens.

What is a body? Asking this question through the lens of your lived experience is a call to remember the gentle yet radical presence of living tissue. It is a call to consider the possibility that this radical presence has a place and purpose in the wider scope of life on earth. And it brings up the certainty that, as a human, you are interacting with this living entity—this living process that happens to be called (in English) a *body*—at all times.

Although the word *body* appears in this book, we are mindful of the many layers of meaning that surround and infuse this word, and we use other terms that open up new contexts for the experience of living in one's body.

The body is a living organism. Living organisms take in energy to maintain themselves, to grow, and to complexify. A living organism acts as a whole. It exists on an evolutionary continuum. Every organism is a living process, nested within and always in relationship to the larger, living context of its ecosystem.

The body is a fluid system. Fluids move in patterns of waves, arcs, spirals, curves, pulses, and circulatory currents. The character of water, the primary fluid in the body, is to transform. Water is mutable, capable of dissolving into turbulence and seeming formlessness, then coalescing into new form, taking the shape of its container. The characteristics of water are profoundly enmeshed within the structures, movements, and life cycles of living organisms. Water is essential to all life on earth.

The body is a process, an unfolding space-time "happening," the piece of the universe that happens to be available to you through your own embodied experience. The body can be understood as a creative process, at its essence always arriving, always moving, always changing. In this sense, *the body is movement*.

Throughout your practice sessions, the question *what is a body?* becomes w*hat is* this *body, in my experience of it now?* Your experience at any moment may be affected by your history, culture, and immediate situation, and yet, in the realm of practice it is possible to dive below the surface to discover other dimensions of meaning. The ongoing, changing quality of experience keeps this question open and allows for evolving answers. As a moving inquiry, the body's actual potential expands beyond the limits of any fixed definition.

ELEMENTS OF PRACTICE AND THE ROLE OF INQUIRY

The movement practice offered here may be described as an inquiry into the following five elements:
- attention
- breath
- sound
- movement
- sensation

More specifically, this practice involves inquiring into the *movement* of each element—*the movement* of attention, of breath, of sound, of movement, of sensation—with the intent of nourishing your life force. These five elements are not isolated components; rather, they offer you places to begin to participate with subtler levels of movement. For each element, the question goes back to: how is this moving—how is this changing—and how is my relationship to it and my awareness of it changing?

At a very fundamental level, movement is change and change is movement. How you participate with change is a choice you make on a moment-to-moment basis. Consider your *attention:* on the one hand, you can "direct" your attention toward something, and on the other, you can be aware of your attention as it shifts. Over time, you may be able to do both simultaneously. Similarly, with *breath*, you can control your breathing in various ways and you can also attune, receptively, to the particular texture and movement of each breath.

Sound, here meaning vocalization accompanying breath, highlights the movement of breath through the body's tissues and enhances the subtler levels of movement there. You can "make" sound and you can also notice the effects of vocalization. Sound can penetrate dense tissue as well as dense meanings that one holds around experiences of tension, discomfort, and fear.

Movement is always going on in the body, whether you are directing it or discerning the ever more refined levels of undirected movement that occur. At these levels, the movement of *sensation* comes alive and is integral to the feedback you get from your practice.

To be in a moving inquiry is to widen the lens of your awareness and become curious about your experience. Inquiry is a state of mind, an open-ended way of participating with the fluid process that is your body. Inquiry involves suspending what you know and what you think you know about yourself, your body, and what is going to happen next. It is choosing to open, to the degree of your current capability, to the unknown.

PRACTICE SEQUENCE

Breaths in this sequence:
- Lunar Breath
- M Sound

What follows is a basic sequence incorporating the five elements to practice now and during the coming week.

Every practice session invites you to pause before you fully dive into it. In the pause, let your inquiry take form with whatever is present in you now. Consider, if you like, *what is it I am in partnership with, here at this moment?* Allow your own definitions of "body" to come up, during and after your practice.

For this three-part sequence, consider a first exploration of about ten minutes; you may find it helpful to use a timer. We suggest you go through the segments in the order given, taking more or less time in each segment, as you choose. If you complete all three segments within the ten-minute time frame, simply begin again. When you have completed the time, gently bring your exploration to a close.

Resting in relative stillness, notice what is arising in your experience. Then take a few minutes to write down notes for yourself. Record some of what you experienced, which might include particular sensations, insights that came to you, and responses to your initial inquiry.

1. *Lunar Breath:*

Begin in a sitting position. (Alternatively, you may do this lying down on your back.)

The *lunar breath* is a soft, subtle breath that you can do almost anywhere, at home or in public. Here, we use it with a sense of a gentle wave traveling over and through your whole body. The breath evokes the soft, indistinct way your body might appear under the light of the moon (hence the name "lunar"). One way of thinking about this breath is that it diffuses edges and softens boundaries.

To do the lunar breath, begin with your mouth closed. After a normal inhalation through your nose, exhale very, very gently, letting the breath slide along the back of your throat. There is a slight yet audible sound, like the sound of the ocean in a seashell. Try this for five to eight breaths. Then pause, noticing what is arising in your felt experience.

2. *M Sound:*

The second piece in this sequence brings in sound and touch. Remaining seated (or lying down), place your hands gently on your chest at the level of the heart. Inhale normally with your mouth closed. On exhalation, mouth still closed, hum the letter *M*, following the breath and sound to the end. As you repeat the sound, notice its vibratory effect and how the vibrations move. You may begin to notice that you can guide the sound to particular areas of your body or let it move freely. Allow the movement of the M sound to spiral, circulate, and penetrate inside your body, especially in the region of your heart and sternum under your hands. Experiment with the M sound for three breaths, taking your time between each breath.

As you continue to make the M sound, you may sense vibrations moving through different layers of tissue. Try placing your hands elsewhere on your neck and torso, repeating the M sound one to three times in each location and noticing what you experience and how the sound moves. You may also wish to experiment with bringing sound and touch to another area, perhaps one that is tense or highlighted to you in some way, noticing if and how the sensation in that area shifts.

To complete this segment, pause again, noticing any continuing sensation of reverberation.

3. *Lateral Drifting:*

The last piece of this sequence introduces movement. You may continue sitting or come onto all fours—on your knees and forearms. Beginning with the M sound again, gently add a slow, lateral (sideways) movement through the ribs. Imagine the movement of seaweed and feel your spine being drawn into a slow, undulating motion out to one side, then coming back to the center. Allow the movement to unfold very slowly, guided by the movement of your breathing, rather than "doing" it mechanically.

This movement is called "drifting" because there is no particular direction. It varies randomly each time, drifting to one side, then back towards the center, then to the other side. The fluid process of your breathing introduces its own subtle, slightly undulatory, variations into the basic intention of lateral movement. Gradually, you may sense movement spreading into the limbs and the rest of the body.

As you sound and drift, allow your attention to reside inside the movement. That is, instead of watching the movement from above and directing it, let your attention become immersed in the movement—the movement of movement—and the sensations arising from movement.

To complete the sequence, gently bring your movement to a close. Pause for several minutes to notice changes, or whatever is arising, in your felt experience. Then take a few moments to write your notes.

PRACTICE AND JOURNALING

Assignment 1: Practice at least one or more times during the next seven days. First, take the time to set up your practice space if you have not already done so. Then use your practice space and this basic practice sequence as a starting point. We suggest thirty minutes as a general guideline if you are just starting out.

Assignment 2: As you practice this week, inquire into the sense of *nourishment*. What is the feeling of nourishment to you? How do you recognize and respond to it? When and where do you experience it?
How do you nourish yourself? How can the sounds and/or movements nourish you?

Assignment 3: Over the course of the week, notice and write down your responses to the following
- How is this way of moving different from other movement modalities you have experienced?
- Imagine and describe how this way of practicing might fit into your daily life.
- Notice if and how inquiry comes into your daily life.

THE MOON

Willingness to hold the moon infinite
In its golden round body

Riding the low continuous sound
That holds variation
Generous in its nature
To change

They say they want change
And yet they get out of bed every morning
With the same train of trumping thoughts
Going through their heads

A soundless existence
And we have this
A body, whole and full
Always working to somehow keep us well
Heart beating

Use those beats for something good
Let the pause between them change you
Let the rim of your life glass
Shimmy with possibility
Feel the condensation drip down
The inside of your skin
And drink

Explore the seam on the other side of your mattress
Let your feet dangle off the strange edge of difference

Inhale the side of the world that's not yours
Learn
Feel
Dignify in this newness

Let your hand be shaped like a cup
Those on the other side can drink from it
The handle, your heart beating and pausing
To see all the colors of all the eyes everywhere

Willingness to hold
Hold willingly

—Bobbie Ellis

WEEK 2

SETTING UP THE EXPERIMENT

Sacred listening is leaning in softly with the willingness to be changed.
—Mark Nepo

CENTERING

Find a comfortable place to sit or lie down. Notice the inner shift that occurs as you go from whatever you were doing before to what you are experiencing now. Notice how it feels at a sensory level to be here.

As you survey your interior landscape, you may become aware of the flow of gravity connecting you to the ground. You may become aware of your breathing, small movements within your body, the sounds in the room and beyond.

Pause here for several breath cycles before moving on. As you wait in the stream of experience, allow yourself to open and receive whatever is occurring, without judging or trying to push or pull yourself in any particular direction.

PRUE JEFFRIES, *Duck Glide*

Take one last look around the interior landscape, and then, gently, begin to open your eyes.

THE LABORATORY

In this chapter we outline a framework which incorporates the elements of attention, breath, sound, movement, and sensation in a sequence that enables you to participate with them in a variety of ways.

At the heart of this movement practice is an inquiry into human flourishing. You are designing and furnishing the laboratory of your personal movement experiment. What occurs in this laboratory has to do with recognizing, engaging with, and learning about that sense of flourishing. You are continually being invited into curiosity about your own felt experience and what enlivens it.

As inquiry, this approach to practice is different from others in an important way: there is no "outside" instruction. There are no particular positions or movements to study, memorize, and perfect. Many people are accustomed to having someone tell them exactly what to do—where this arm should be, how far the torso should turn, how the gaze should be, and so on. In these circumstances, participants are always in a state of trying to align themselves to an outside authority and trying to "do it right."

In this movement practice, there is a suggested sequence and some practical guidelines, but there is not much more than that. As you practice, you may think, "I don't know if I'm doing it right." Indeed, with no prescribed positions or movements, how are you to know if you are doing it correctly?

In following this approach, you are rediscovering a state of *not being relegated to any outside instruction*. You have the freedom to explore and discover who you are when you are not trying to follow instructions from an outside source. Your movement practice is an inquiry into human flourishing, as it emerges through you. You have only your own senses through which to access it. This is what we mean by *self-referencing*. You attend to and engage with the movement of your own experience and, in doing so, you discover your capacity to know and to nourish yourself.

Self-referencing is about becoming your own authority. You are the only expert on yourself. This is your process; it is no one else's. You do not have to keep up with anyone; your pacing is your own. You are cultivating trust that something will show up to interest or guide you. You are exercising your capacity to tolerate uncertainty. You are practicing acceptance of the full-on sensory experience of being alive. Learning to tend to what nourishes you moment-by-moment is a fundamental life skill.

SETTING UP THE EXPERIMENT

Below we give the basic outline of a practice session, introducing terms in *italics* that encapsulate some of the components of this approach.

Consider your practice session as a somatic "experiment" running roughly like this:
- Notice how you are feeling at the start.
- Engage in a prepared *sequence* of breath, sound and movement.
- Notice how you are feeling at the end. Ask, "What is arising? What has changed?"

- Repeat the sequence three times, pausing after each round. We call this kind of repetition *layering*, to acknowledge that each time through the sequence there are differences in how you feel while doing it and in how your tissues respond.
- Write or draw for several minutes to record something about your experience.

What follows is a more in-depth description of each phase of the practice session.

CHECKING YOUR BASELINE

At the outset of the sequence, you take note of your starting point, a *baseline* against which change can be measured. Sitting or lying down, you refrain from movement and listen into your felt experience without judgement. We call this *open attention*.

Open attention is a practice of regarding your own experience without preference and without trying to change it. This pause to take in your felt experience is as important to the process of inquiry as the "doing" involved in making sound, working with breath, and initiating movement. When you intentionally make a breath or sound, you introduce vibration into your tissues; when you pause, you listen for the effects of that vibration and the possibility of a response in the tissues. "Doing" and "listening" alternate in a kind of call-and-response pattern. A large part of your practice is to cultivate open attention—unbiased awareness—simply by pausing from time to time to receive your sensations, however they present themselves.

To take your baseline, you may ask yourself several questions, while remaining in open attention.

- *How and where is my body meeting the ground? What is the degree of lift in my body holding me away from the ground? How much effort is there in my body meeting the ground?*
- *How is my breath moving? Where do I feel it in my body? What is the song of my breath at this moment? What is it saying to me?*
- *What is the quality of my attention? What is dominant in my awareness? Are there any specific areas of my body that are calling for attention?*

At the end of the sequence, when you return to your baseline, you may ask these same questions again as you gauge the effect of the sequence on your state of being. Remember, though, that these questions are simply guidelines for you to use. There may be others that come to you at any given time. The intent of the pause is to notice what is arising in your felt experience. The invitation is to feel what is alive within you.

FIRST ROUND: SHIFTING THE CONTEXT

As you go through the sequence for the first time, you are gently shifting the context from the outer, every-day, culturally-organized world around you to the inner, more formless world of your felt, lived body.

The first round draws your attention toward the level and quality of your sense of effort. Human beings, as living organisms, have an exquisite capacity to adapt to the fast pace and pressure of modern life. This adaptation comes from a survival instinct, yet it can diminish your life force if it is not interrupted on a regular basis.

The way your tissues organize to cope with the stress of life creates your familiar state of being, the context for your everyday life. It is common for this familiar state, with its readiness to respond to demands, to carry over into your movement practice. This is why, as you begin, you are invited to pause, to breathe, to move, and to inquire. When you enter a process of inquiry, your muscular effort changes as a whole, in effect shifting your context of moving and being.

This shift in context heightens awareness of your habitual ways of moving. Perhaps your movement feels a little stiff and awkward, rather than flowing and harmonious. You might experience heaviness, tension, a sense of bumping into old habits, or a sense of discombobulation. Rather than trying to make flow happen or impose harmony, simply notice what you feel.

SECOND ROUND: INTERRUPTING HABITS

As you repeat the sequence a second time, you start to let breath and movement speak to the habits. By allowing yourself to simply notice what is occurring, you make room for a sense of choice between staying in the familiar context or probing what is underneath the habits.

To interrupt your habits, you might lengthen the pauses between a series of breaths/sounds or move very, very slowly—so slowly that it is as if the flow of movement were broken into tiny granules. Between the granules, a tiny point of space opens in which you can make a choice—for example, to change direction ever so slightly, or to see where in your body you can let go of tension, or to wait for the next inhalation. To become aware of the choice point is to break your habitual pattern. It may help to bring to mind the sensation of nourishment as you know it and the possibility that small changes feed a living system in ways that the repetition of habits cannot.

THIRD ROUND: THE EMERGING UNEXPECTED

Now you enter the third round, repeating the sequence once again. When you let go of the habits of holding, you free up the vital energy that was being used to maintain your familiar adaptive patterns. As you do this, you may be aware of more sensation, more subtle movement, more breath, and more feeling of aliveness than you have experienced before. All these inform your organism, possibly through unexpected sensory channels (a flush of warmth, for example, or a sense of lightness), surprising imagery, or unplanned possibilities of movement. You may have the sense of arriving in a completely new configuration.

Notice how you *participate* with what is newly arising. When you get a sense of something coming forth, see if you can suspend the tendency to direct it in any way. Rather than predicting or "doing," you open to the possibility that whatever is arising is an expression of health, wholeness, and fluidity.

BETWEEN THE ROUNDS

You begin and end the sequence with open attention as part of your baseline, and you also pause in open attention *between* the layers. After each round, you come back to your starting position to pause in the relative rest and stillness of open attention. You also may go into open attention at any point in the sequence to simply become more aware of what is occurring within your body.

Resting between the rounds allows you to assimilate new information. You take note of what has changed, however subtly. It may be as simple as, my belly feels a little looser, or—I feel like more of my body is in contact with the ground. This pause allows you to register and value the new sensations, forge new connections throughout your organism, and signal another way of being. This new awareness becomes a resource for the future.

PRACTICE SEQUENCE

New breaths in this sequence:
- Hah Breath
- M Sound

1. *Baseline/Open Attention:*

Choose a neutral position, such as sitting or lying on your back, to take your baseline. Ask yourself what position would feel nourishing to you right now. If you are not sure, just pick a starting position to begin with for today.

2. *Hah Breath:*

The Hah breath is a relaxed and elongated release of exhalation, like a long sigh of relief or contentment: "Haaahhhh." Inhale through your nose. Relax your jaw, open your mouth, and exhale through your mouth with a soft release of the sound "Haaahhhh." Allow a feeling of floating, as if you were buoyed up by a large body of water or an inflated raft.

Repeat this breath three times. Take your time, relaxing further with each soft exhale.

3. *M Sound:*

Inhale through your nose. On exhalation, mouth still closed, hum the letter *M*, following the exhalation and sound to the end.

Repeat this breath three times. As you repeat the sound, notice its vibratory effect and how the vibrations move through your body. Try resting your hands on your chest, abdomen, or face, to feel how the sound moves.

4. *Lateral Drifting with the M Sound:*

Make the M sound again as you exhale, this time gently adding a *slow, lateral (sideways) movement* through your ribs. Imagine the movement of seaweed and feel your spine being drawn into a slow, undulating motion out to one side, then coming back to the center.

Repeat this five to seven times. Allow the movement to unfold on its own, differently each time, and let it be guided by the movement of your breath rather than by "doing" it mechanically.

5. *Movement Exploration:*

Allow the lateral drifting motion to take you further off center. Move slowly, pausing from time to time and attending with a sense of exploration to the changing sensations and internal movements that arise. As you go further, you can bring in the M sound or Hah breath occasionally, noticing if and how the sound supports your movement. Continuing for several minutes or even longer, allow the exploration to take you into new configurations.

This kind of unplanned, open-ended movement exploration may sometimes arise on its own, and it can also be initiated intentionally. Either way, it is an integral part of movement practice, which we discuss in a later chapter. This improvisational aspect of the practice sequence mirrors the innovation at the heart of life. Open movement is where the body reveals its intelligence, moving so as to heal itself when healing is needed. Aligning with the body's native fluidity, you can begin to trust in something larger than yourself.

As you proceed through each round of the sequence, your sense of weight may begin to shift and lighten. The elongation and buoyancy of the exhale in the Hah breath may alter the felt quality of your movement, as if fluid circulating throughout your torso and limbs were the source of movement. The vibrational quality of the M sound may travel throughout your body and awaken new movements. And the lateral drifting may lead you into new directions in the space around you.

6. *Return to Your Baseline:*

To draw your movement exploration to a close, move gently back to your baseline position. Pause for several minutes in open attention. Notice what sensations are arising. What is the quality of your breathing? How is your body meeting the ground?

PRACTICE AND JOURNALING

Assignment 1: The best way to get a feel for the practice is to study with a teacher in a live setting. You can also find videos online (search for "Continuum videos") that offer another way to get familiar with the kind of movement we are encouraging. These videos are not to show you what your practice should look like. Movement manifests very differently in different people, and differently in the same person in different contexts.

Rather, consider what you are aware of in your own body as you watch the movement. How does it affect your breathing? What sensations, thoughts, or feelings come up? What do you see happening here?

Assignment 2: In your practice during the next week, allow enough time to layer the sequence three times. Then describe in writing something about your experience, referring to your physical sensations, mental imagery, and/or thoughts. What changes did you notice on successive layers?

Assignment 3: During the week, notice how the practice is affecting your day-to-day life. Ideally, make notes about your experience several times during the week. Did you notice less tension in your body? More ease? Was there a situation in which you were more aware of your familiar way of responding than before, or in which you were able to respond differently? If so, describe the experience, briefly or at length, as you are called.

WISTERIA

Winter again transforms the green to gold—
Leaves hanging, weighted and weary
After another storm.
Yet roots hold steady through the years,
Deep in dark ground,
Intimately wound to their place of belonging.
Branches quiver with rain,
Bend with wind…

But what of the trellis?
Strong curling Wisteria wood woven in and through the openings—
Growth could not happen without the spaces for climbing.
She cannot thrive without support.
The structure allows her blossoms to be seen
In full glory as Spring arrives.
They would quietly mix with earth and disappear too soon
 without the steady presence of the trellis.

This human life is rich with storm.
We weave together, one to another, to find our growing path
To steady ourselves and touch new heights—without breaking!
We find the open spaces, where the urging on of mysterious life forces
Can partner with us in our emerging and changing,
Allowing blossoming of each season to
Lead us towards radical transformations—
Unexpected, startling, terrifying and rejuvenating all at once!

May we remember, in each moment, the tiny possibility of great things:
The seeds of quiet joy and uninhibited laughter, the tears of gratitude and grief, the breath and blessing of being alive today, just as it is.
May we cultivate open space, ease and rest—
Alone and together,
For we could not grow without the presence of one another
In our infinite variety and exuberant color.

—Beth Pettengill Riley

WEEK 3

AMPLIFYING YOUR PRACTICE

Change arrives in nature when time has ripened.... To change is one of the great dreams of every heart—to change the limitations, the sameness, the banality, the pain.... Ask yourself: At which threshold am I now standing?
—John O'Donahue

CENTERING

Sitting or lying down, let your awareness settle within the boundaries of your body. Begin to focus on your breathing. As you follow a full cycle of inhalation and exhalation, take in the sensations that arrive one after the other: the touch of air on the inner surfaces of your nose, the movement of your abdomen and chest, the many small movements your body. Let the belly release; let the jaw release.

Allow yourself to be touched by your own experience. Sensations arise, change, subside. You may notice the edges of emotions and memories attached to certain sensations. For now, you can choose not to get involved with them. Rather, stay closely connected to the process of breathing, noticing the nuances of change with each breath cycle.

BARBARA MINDELL, *Contrast Peace: Open Attention*

Now, prepare to offer yourself the sound of M. Bring your hands to a place on your body, such as your face, your heart, your abdomen, or another place that seems to call for touch. Inhale normally and then, on the exhalation, make the sound of M, following the sound to the end of the outbreath. Repeat this two more times. Then pause for a few more minutes, taking in any sensations that arise.

CHANGE AS A DOORWAY

The focus of this week is introducing variation into your practice. There are several reasons to introduce change:
- to meet the innate need for novelty in your body as a living system;
- to experience new sensations, rather than stay within your familiar realm;
- to increase your adaptive "fitness," your ability to adjust to new circumstances quickly;
- to break out of habitual physical and cultural patterning on every level;
- to explore both personal and evolutionary potential.

The subtle variability found throughout nature signifies a kind of built-in creativity, an innovative responsiveness to ongoing change in an organism's environment. Change is always occurring in the natural world; no two breaths are exactly alike, just as no two waves are exactly alike.

Variation in movement offers essential nourishment, vital to an organism's health. The modern cultural context vastly reduces the range of what is considered acceptable in terms of breath, sound, and movement. In the context of your practice, however, you can in a harmonious way set up circumstances that offer or even compel variation. By intentionally and gently introducing variation, you push the edges of your "normal" range and increase the range of choices available to you. To meet your edge and enter your *dis*comfort zone—this is how you expand your capability on a physical level, which is likely to affect your life as a whole.

In addition, through exploring the almost endless possible variations, you are not simply engaging in your private movement experience but you are also innovating the possibilities of *human* experience. Your discoveries contribute not only to your personal world but also to larger social and evolutionary processes.

All of this is developing your innate capacity to explore new circumstances, build resilience throughout your physicality, and find pleasure in meeting the unknown.

A basic characteristic of life is to complexify. Living systems are designed to take in energy from their environment and use it not only to grow and reproduce, but also to adapt and learn, thus complexifying their internal structures or behaviors, or both. Insofar as breath and sound increase the body's fluidity, variations in breath and sound serve to complexify the fluid state. As you enrich your practice with new qualities of breath and movement, increasingly nuanced sensory information begins to surface in your conscious awareness. Such embodied awareness, in turn, expands the choices available to you in "real life."

WAYS OF INTRODUCING CHANGE

1. *Changing Orientation to Gravity.*

One means of introducing movement variation involves changing your body's orientation in the gravitational field. To do this you simply change your starting position on each successive round of the sequence. For example, if your first round began in a sitting position, the second could begin on hands and knees. The third could begin lying down on your back or a return to the sitting position. With each round, you follow the same basic sequence of breath, sound, and movement, making adjustments as needed and noticing differences in sensation.

Intentional changes in your starting position invite variation into your movements by offering access to substantial, often-new, somatic information:

- Different positions, at a gross level, give weight-bearing responsibility to different parts of the body while freeing other parts—often in unexpected ways.
- Changing the body's relationship within the gravitational field affects the circulation of fluids and other body systems, producing new sensations.
- Different orientations challenge the body's fluid system to adapt and thus extend your adaptive range—that is, you become more resilient.
- Moving from a different orientation allows you to undo the unstated cultural assumption that the upright, forward-facing orientation is normal, correct, and optimal.
- You tune into patterns of orientation and movement shared with other animal species, enabling you to explore what is possible for the human body to be and do.

As you continue to practice over time, you will encounter an array of starting positions. A folding chair offers a great variety of potential starting points. Props like yoga bolsters, physioballs, and foam rollers—as well as household furniture, walls, and counters—hold endless possibilities for exploration.

When starting in a new position, the process is generally the same. First, you allow several minutes to notice changes occurring simply as a result of the new orientation. Then you begin the sequence. If you are elevated or inverted (say, on a chair), it is important to move slowly, always aware of where your weight is supported and balanced.

2. *Varying Speed and Intensity*

A second way of introducing change involves varying the speed and intensity of the breaths, sounds, and movements of the sequence. Your system is capable of a dynamic range that runs from slow to fast, steady to random/irregular, gentle to forceful. You have already practiced with slow, steady breaths (the lunar breath, the M sound, the O breath), as well as with the encouragement to move very, very slowly. This slowness counteracts the high speed of modern life, helps you to let go of physical and emotional tension, and opens the door to subtle sensation. At the other end of the spectrum you will encounter breaths that are rapid, percussive, and/or vibratory, as well as movements that are quick, loose, or forceful. When you practice with these qualities intentionally, they have an invigorating effect and prepare you to meet demanding situations with greater finesse and fluidity than before.

Ways of incorporating variation into your practice include:

- juxtaposing dynamically different breaths and sounds in a sequence;
- alternating fast and slow movement (say, in thirty-to-sixty-second intervals);
- varying the rhythm and/or intensity of a particular breath or sound;
- pausing between breaths or at random times as you go through the sequence;
- adding resistance (wrist or ankle weights, for example) during one round, leading to a sense of release and fresh capacity for exploration when the weight is removed on the next round;
- self-touch—to bring awareness to particular places on the body or intensify the experience of a sound or breath;
- focusing intention and effort so as to explore outside your familiar dynamic range.

As you proceed over time, you expand your repertoire of breaths and sounds, as well as kinds and qualities of movement. You discover new responses in your essentially fluid system, enriching and refining your capacity to meet new circumstances with discernment. You become increasingly receptive and expressive as a member of the natural world. The potential outcome is to experience a greater capacity of flourishing in the human body than would otherwise be available to you.

PRACTICE SEQUENCE

New breaths in this sequence:
- Jacques
- O Sound
- E Sound

Start in a sitting position or lying on your back.

1. *Os spiraling through midline from tail (coccyx) to cranium.*

As with the M sound, you make the O sound on exhalation. As you say "O," notice the tubular shaping of your mouth. As you make the O sound, visualize the sound vibration moving in the fluid-filled dural tube at the center of your spine. Starting at the pubic bone, use touch to follow the sound as it travels up the midline. Picture the O sound as a fluid current moving upward through the spine in arcs, curves, spirals, and vortices.

2. *Es spreading out from midline at three levels: navel, heart, eyes.*

The E sound, here, introduces *lateral* movement—that is, movement from the midline out to the side.

The E sound follows from the sideways movement of your mouth when you say "E," similar to the movement at the beginning of a smile. Again, inhale normally and make the E sound throughout the exhalation.

Now, place the fingertips of both hands at the navel, and as you make the E sound, draw your hands apart to each side. You may have a sense of the tissues spreading to the side under your fingers. Repeat the sound three times, continuing to draw the hands further apart on each exhalation/sound. You may experience an asymmetrical sideways movement similar to the lateral drift introduced earlier.

Try going back and forth between the E and O sounds to experience the different effects of each sound as well as the effects of using them in combination.

3. *Jacques breath into skin, "wrapping" the body with fingertips touching the skin.*

The Jacques breath blends the sounds of the French "Ja" (as in Jacques) with a "Za" sound, alternating the two in a kind of dynamic play: "Ja Za Ja Za," etc. The highly vibrational Jacques sound can elicit sensation throughout the body's tissues, bathing you in a wash of sound. In this case, as you do the Jacques breath, use the fingertips on the skin as if you were wrapping your torso, limbs, and head. Allow your attention to rotate from making the sound to receiving the sound, to the act of touching, to receiving the sensation of the touch, and around again.

4. *Open attention.*

Think of this as harvesting the effects of the sound and touch that you have just introduced.

5. *Movement exploration.*

After two or more rounds of breath, sound, touch, and movement, you may sense a readiness to move in new ways—and if so, after a pause feel free to do so.

6. *Return to baseline.*

PRACTICE AND JOURNALING

Assignment 1: Practice this sequence at least two times this week and notice the differences in your experience each time. Allow enough time to layer the sequence three times.

Suggestion: Begin the first round lying down. On the second round, begin sitting. On the third round, return to lying down. Note your sensations.

If your time is limited, use one of the new breaths instead of all three, or follow the basic practice (lunar breath, M sound, and lateral drifting) for five to ten minutes, two times this week.

Assignment 2: Become an observer of variation, in nature and elsewhere in your surroundings. Watch for variations in sound, movement, visual, or tactile landscapes. Make notes about what you observe.

Assignment 3: Respond to the following questions in writing:
- How did your organism respond to the change in orientation to gravity?
- How did your organism respond to the new breaths/sounds?
- Describe some of your physical sensations or imagery. Note any insights or questions that occurred to you.

TWO SIDES (CONTINUUM CLASS 1-4-14)

My right side has the winter blues.
While the left side flits and flirts, meandering away endlessly,
my right hip is not so sure…
Faintly, underneath a landscape of snow, rumbles a current.
It cannot hide its palpable power,
this crystallized memory of my fascia.
I sense you, father memory pushed down,
you have been safe there for years, maybe eons.
I know you have the potential to lift mountains!

But first patience is needed: more puffed o's down limbs,
into feet propped on chair.
Listening, waiting, following,
a hairline crack from hip to feet,
spells out first hesitant lines,
unclear without substance.

Then…suddenly…I stand on a chair as if on new ground.

Another chapter opens like lips, expectant.
The looong thigh slide becomes sweet, murmuring meditation –
until the need to stretch in opposite directions takes over,
fibers fierce and taut,
as if on a rack—
the great tension felt in love,
before two can become one.

Our winter breath is a bear at the height of hibernation.
"What else is stirring?" Nothing stirs.
We are in our caves, dreaming,
  allowing two sides to follow the scent of spring.

The spell breaks with a laugh and we're back,
in a world where we can drive our cars home,
where children await to tug us into their worlds,
where trash needs to be taken out and the dishwasher emptied,
where our pains return like vultures and computers lure the
mind and stifle the body.
The cave forgotten, lost amid split hair ends.

—Sandra Capellaro

WORKING ON THE CHAIR

A sturdy, armless chair can be used in innumerable ways to put the body in a new—or less familiar—orientation to the pull of gravity as a starting point for movement exploration.

Some examples:
- You begin lying on the floor with your lower legs elevated, resting on the seat of the chair.
- You begin seated on the chair. (Admittedly, this is not a "new" position, but you can work with it in new ways.)
- "Side-entry" (see photo): your pelvis and torso are supported across the seat of the chair; your lower arm extends to the floor, supporting your upper chest; and your legs and feet are free.

No matter how you begin, the way to proceed is basically the same. The most important principles are to *go slowly* and *always be aware of where your "ground" is*—that is, where you are supported.

1. Settle yourself securely in a starting position that you can hold for several minutes.

    Note: If your intention is to use the side entry, before you settle take a few minutes to patiently experiment with the placement of your hips and torso on the chair, so that the

One possible way of working on the chair

pressure on your arm/shoulder is not too great and your neck is not pinched. You may need to allow more of your body's weight to be carried by the chair than you thought, at least at first. Apply a gentle pulsing motion through your arm, as if it were a conduit of gravitational flow into the ground and back up into your body, with a rebounding effect. In motion, your body makes small adjustments, sometimes like a key in a lock, seeking out an arrangement that "unlocks" greater movement potential. Keep your first forays with the side entry quite limited in time in response to your experience, strain, or muscle fatigue. Change sides. Know that you will return, that you are awakening little-used musculature, and that this is a learning process occurring through the conversation between your sensation and "you".

Now, settle yourself securely in a starting position (such as seated on the chair) that you can hold for several minutes. You can go back into the side entry exploration after taking the following preparatory steps.

2. Pause to feel, quite consciously, where and how you are supported. Allowing your weight to sink into the places of support, make tactile connection—even pressing lightly through your hands/feet to the chair or ground, as appropriate. Pause also to notice how this position is affecting the direction and movement of fluid in your system. Take in any sensations arising simply as a result of being in this new orientation.

3. Relate to the chair as a living partner. This is a shift of consciousness that may take a few minutes. You could imagine the chair as an animal with its own sentience. Imagine its willingness, even desire, to interact with you in a supportive way. You bring to this meeting a certain respect and caution, feeling your way with a new person/being, allowing trust to develop gradually.

4. Begin your sequence of breath and sound in this starting position, infusing your system with the subtle, fluid-stimulating effects of conscious breathing and sound vibration. At completion of the breath/sound sequence, pause briefly before moving on.

5. Now begin to move slowly, always aware of where and how you are supported. As you explore further from your most stable position, remain attentive to your body's ways of keeping you safe from falling or overstressing certain joints. Pause as often as desired to take in the sensations that arise as you enter into new configurations. Small movements—smaller than you thought—may bring the greatest flow of sensation.

6. Allow this to be a process of discovery. For example, you may find that pressing down in one area enables another to lift easily. New areas take the responsibility of holding the body's weight, allowing other areas to move freely.

7. Do not push beyond your limits. You may go through several rounds, keeping the timings short (especially at first), and changing position so as to avoid overdoing it on one side or in a particular area. Be alert to avoid the conventional exercise mindset of "pushing" to reach specific goals and try to stay within the fluid atmosphere of self-nourishment and exploration. Remember the tendency within animal intelligence for exploration for its

own sake (think octopi), and the love of play (dolphins, primates, children). Rightly enjoy the strength in your system, the confidence of extending in space in completely new ways, the magic of connected flow within your system, the sheer fullness of being.

8. At the end of your exploration, rest for several minutes in a neutral position. (This may be lying down, seated, or standing—depending on how you began and what you intend to do next.) Follow the internal sensations of coming back into a familiar orientation to gravity before moving on.

For reasons of safety as well as to maximize the benefits of the chair, we cannot overemphasize the value of working with an experienced Continuum teacher, especially one with experience in using the chair and other means to extend and explore the capacity for movement in all possible orientations to gravity.

WEEK 4

MOVING BEYOND THE CONTAINER

*What a wonder
it must be to move
from tight encasement
of seed
to a form pushing down,
reaching up,
taking into the senses
the feel and support
of the darkness
below
the pull of the light and rain
above
the calling up, the invitation
down and deep*

—Raine Brown, excerpt from
"The Soil of Myself"

SATYA KIRSCH, *Spilling Light 3*

CENTERING

Sit and take a moment to notice where you are, the sense of space around you, the sense of ground supporting you. Allow your joints to soften, releasing effort at ever more subtle levels.

Take each question in turn, allowing one or two breath cycles before moving on to the next:
　What impressions are you receiving visually, whether your eyes are open or closed?
　What is coming to you through the sense of hearing?
　What do you notice through the senses of smell and taste?
　What is coming to you through the sensations on your skin?

Now, notice your breathing, its pace, depth, variation, or texture.

Take one low, long, lingering O sound. Let the sound permeate all the tissues in your body. Pause to feel the effect of sound in your tissues.

Then, letting go of the act of sounding, remain present in the wake of the sound vibrations. Return your attention again to your breathing, noticing any dimension of the breath that may have changed. Attend to your experience without evaluation or judgment.

Slowly, gently, open your eyes and return to the space you are in.

THE SEQUENCE IS THE CONTAINER

With this handbook as your guide, you are creating a "container," a kind of space that is secure enough and yet open enough to meet yourself, experiment, and explore. In a more conventional framework, the container might be the room where you practice or a studio where you take class, replete with its own set of expectations and conditions. Here, the container at its most basic level is the *sequence* you choose to follow. The breaths and sounds, the movements patterns, and the intentional variations in orientation to gravity and intensity—these components and their ordering create the container of this practice. You make conscious choices in the design of your container.

Before you move beyond the container, you practice within it. In doing so, you become intimate with subtle variations within yourself occurring moment by moment. The layers of breath and sound gradually build a vibratory resonance within your tissues. Following the sequence gives you a background against which to be aware of the many ways you limit your own movement. You strengthen your capacity to feel what is nourishing and to respond with freshness. The sequence, along with your practice space and time, offers you both the safety and the freedom in which to develop, honor, and empower the voice of your own body. Layering the sequence through several rounds serves as a consciously orchestrated preparation for the moment when you may find yourself hovering on the edge between the container and uncharted territory.

MOVING BEYOND THE CONTAINER

It is in the nature of genuine inquiry to ask, what lies beyond? At the end of the third round of the sequence, you return to your baseline and go into open attention. This time, you drop the agenda of following the sequence and simply tune into whatever is happening in your system. What calls you now? Where do you feel a new aliveness? What do you do when all the instructions have dropped away? Perhaps you feel a subtle urge to sound or move. You initiate a small movement, and through your participation with it, you discover that it "takes off" as if on its own. It is like a dance of listening, receiving, responding—over and over, with variations each time.

You may find that it is possible to *follow* the movement rather than direct it. This *open movement* is a kind of improvisation built in to the practice and one of the ways it differs from "set" practices, like yoga and martial arts.

Why is this of value?

The capacity for innovation builds as the system complexifies through the rounds of breath, sound, and movement. To experience innovation through movement it is necessary to let go of outside instructions and what has become familiar. In doing so, it becomes possible to more fully realize the potential of the entire system. Moving with a sense of open-ended inquiry can take the body into new configurations and unwind dysfunctional patterns. The ability to follow this process fosters trust in the intelligence of the body. It encourages a deep sense of autonomy that is linked to the fundamental creativity of living systems.

Being at the edge of what you know invites you to innovate from the raw material of your individual potential. In entering the uncharted territory "beyond the container," you are also exploring the full range of human capacity in terms of movement and sensation. How can the body move? What sensations can it experience? What is learned in these dimensions of movement, shape, and sensation? How is human knowledge and capability extended by spending time in these new realms of experience?

Here, although you still reside within the container of the culture of modern society, your practice is an opportunity to create a new context for yourself, a context that is open-ended, exploratory, and—as it awakens awareness of the body as a living process—connected to the billion-year-old process of life on earth.

WAYS OF EXPLORING BEYOND THE CONTAINER

Pause. The pause is a form of open attention, an act of dropping effort, intention, and tracking. It creates an opening in the container of the sequence. In the midst of practice, it serves as a moment to ask, how can I move in a different way, and is movement arising on its own?

Pausing allows you to receive the information coming through your felt experience. For example, the Centering at the beginning of this chapter invited you to do just one O sound and then take a full pause. Doing ten O's in a row would have another effect. By pausing you can notice what takes place after making the sound. A pause for a full breath cycle (or two, or even more) allows subtler movements, quieter sensations, and a greater variety of textures and tones to reveal themselves than would otherwise be the case.

Change your quality of movement. We have talked about interrupting patterns of movement. More deeply, it is possible to inquire into your habitual *quality* of movement.

Most people have a familiar "tone," a level of force (or lack thereof) that they exert in most everything they do. This zone of familiarity is part of your identity. To call it your "comfort zone" is accurate if you recognize that it might also be your zone of familiar *dis*comfort.

The first step is to notice what is actually happening. For example, you may find that you are used to "pushing" into life in a certain way, with a certain force. Perhaps you are used to feeling a high degree of urgency about everything you do. The next step is to ask what would happen if you let that tone soften? It could feel refreshing or challenging. By interrupting your quality of movement, you can enter a larger identity with greater choice in your responses to a variety of situations.

Make a small change in direction and/or speed to alter the predictable path of a certain gesture. You might be moving your hand in a particular direction (say, outward from your body), and you already have a thought based on past experience that the hand is going to end up fully extended in the direction it is going. But now you consciously interrupt where you thought it was going. Maybe you simply suspend the movement. Maybe you move it slightly in a new direction. Maybe your speed was steady before, and now you flick your hand. Even the smallest change creates opportunity for something else to emerge out of the movement.

Break symmetry. Introduce asymmetry through your starting position or sequence of movements. For those of us who have studied ballet or modern dance, the dictates of symmetry have a powerful hold on the psyche, creating a tendency to move symmetrically or to expect to duplicate the same movements and sensations on both sides of the body. Notice when and where you have a preference for symmetry and ask: Is there something else to experience here? A curiosity may arise about the different information from each side.

Initiate movement from unfamiliar places in the body. For example, in many contemporary movement and exercise practices the torso is rarely the first place to move. In an effort to maintain stability, people are often told to hold the torso quite static and express movement through the limbs. By developing an awareness of where initiation happens you are opening possibilities for movement innovation.

You can consciously choose random places on the body to move from. During a pause, you might lightly scan your body and allow your interest to alight on a place some distance from where movement was last occurring—the back of your heel, the webbing between two fingers, the middle of your thigh, and so on. There is no need for logic or reasoning here. Trust your imagination and "randomness," which might be body-wisdom in disguise.

Make use of "the accident." Things happen: You roll off your mat. You knock over a glass of water. The dog or the cat is breathing on your face. Or in a class—while you are moving, engaged in your process—you bump somebody else's leg. Do you pull away—assume you made a mistake—lurch out of your process into a state of hypervigilance?

No container is perfectly safe from disturbance. The question is always this: How do I respond and innovate? *How do I move in a different way to engage with whatever is arising*? Unexpected encounters offer the good fortune of real, truly random interruptions to your expectations. Whatever "the accident" is, you can welcome it and choose to innovate. This is the ever-present challenge of living existence, and it can be exciting when you sense yourself meeting it with curiosity, instead of irritation or alarm.

PRACTICE SEQUENCE: EXPLORING POTENT SPACE

The concept of *potent space* comes from the term "negative space" in artwork, referring to the use of empty space around objects or forms. The inquiry in this practice is about attending as much to the spaces inside and around the body as to the tangible structures of the body itself. Ordinarily, you assume that there is "something" (such as your arm) that you are lifting upward with muscular effort, while under your arm there is "nothing." With the suggestion of potent space, you can imagine space as a cushion capable of supporting and lifting your arm. You may feel yourself less dense and more porous than before, capable of being supported and moved by the fullness of space itself.

The sense of potent space may arise on its own, or it may be conjured by a mere suggestion. In either case, it reflects the powerful role that imagination has in shaping how one moves through space and, indeed, in shaping one's entire reality.

Breaths used in this sequence:
- Theta Breath
- O Sound
- E Sound

In this practice sequence we use the *theta breath* to awaken spaces within the body and then explore the space around the body.

The theta breath is related to and slightly different from the "th" sound, as in the word "this." Inhale normally. During your exhalation, the tip of the tongue touches the back of either your top teeth or your bottom teeth (depending on your bite). As you experiment with the pressure of your tongue against the teeth, see if you notice a little cushion of space at the tip of your tongue. You may feel air coming through that cushion of space and also around the sides of your tongue. Try it for three or four breath cycles—inhaling normally, exhaling with the theta breath, following the breath to the end. If doing this creates tension anywhere, try softening your effort a little bit—for instance, in the jaw, the throat, or the pressure of the tongue.

There are many ways to think of the theta breath. One way is to imagine that the breath hits the back of your teeth, ricochets off the teeth, and goes back down inside. Here, the breath is like a sensitive probe for exploring the space inside the throat, the first of the three interior areas we explore in this practice session. If you swallow a few times, you may feel the space within the throat. From there, you may picture the breath spiraling down through esophagus leading into the lungs, the second interior space. The third space is the space at the very top of the legs where the femur bone meets the pelvis.

The proposed sequence is as follows:

1. *Baseline/open attention. Begin sitting on a chair or on a cushion.*

2. *Theta/O into three spaces within the body.*

- Throat: Bring your attention to the back of the throat, and offer the theta breath, three times, into the space there. Allow a pause, then offer the O sound, one time. You may sense that with the theta breath you open up the space from the inside; then, with the O sound, you set up a kind of resonance in and through that space. Allow another pause to "listen" for any sensations and aftereffects of the breath and sound.
- Lungs: Then gently move your attention to the second location, the lungs. Again focusing on either the left or right side, offer the theta breath three times, followed by a pause and the O sound one time, pausing after each to notice what is occurring. Then repeat on the second side.
- Leg/Pelvis Junction: Move your attention to where the top of the leg meets the pelvis. Bring light touch there with your fingertips. Repeat the breath and sound sequence, first on one side, then on the other.

3. *Connecting the internal spaces.*

"Touching" the internal locations with imagination, attention and breath may bring a sense of spaciousness that can spread through the tissues, inviting communication between the spaces. From the inner potent spaces and the connections between them, a kind of coherent, whole-body movement may arise, quite distinct from the sense of moving the tissues *around* the spaces.

4. *Exploring the space around you.*

Begin to lean into the space around you to discover the potency of the space. Slowly take your central axis off of its usual vertical, symmetrical orientation. Moving in small, incremental shifts, allow yourself to feel supported by the space around your body. What changes as you move off the central axis? You may sense micro-adjustments occurring in your tissue to keep you from falling. You may sense support from the "empty" space around you as if it were a flexible cushion that moves you as it expands and contracts. Once you have a felt sense of this support, you can experiment with it by leaning further or lifting a limb to see how far the space will support you.
As you extend yourself into the space around you, experiment with making the sounds of E and O occasionally. You may notice that the sense of potent space, once awakened both internally and externally, is both open and supportive.

5. *Return to baseline.*

To conclude your session, find your way to a pause, go into open attention, and harvest from this practice anything you noticed—perhaps about sensations of nourishment, internal and external space, support, and whatever was new to you. Make notes in your journal.

PRACTICE AND JOURNALING

Assignment 1: Practice at least two times this week (more is great).

Practice allowing enough time to layer the sequence two or three times. If your time is limited, select just one part of the sequence and layer this two or more times. You always have the option of doing the basic practice (lunar breath, M sound, and lateral drifting) for five to ten minutes, two times this week.

Assignment 2: After each practice session, write in response to the following:
- Describe something about your experience, referring to physical sensations, imagery, and/or thoughts that occurred to you.
- Ask yourself: If I truly believed the world supported me, how would my attitude or outlook change?
- What would be the impact of taking into my identity the experience of being part of a larger space or process?

AFTERNOON EMERGENCE (CONTINUUM CLASS 12-7-13)

It's 4 pm and golden sunlight filters into the room, bathing us divers in beauty.
The sun's very disappearance creates a light unmatched by the day's dial.
As I drink in sparkling rays, I ask myself if I would be so bold as to willingly disappear every evening.
Would I rise up in the morning clear and totipotent, freed from the sticky self of yesterday?

There's no standing still in the cycle of nature, even when we refuse our own growth.
Fold and unfold! – I remind myself.
Never stop dancing and you're on the way. Your birth on the pilgrim's journey.

Our eyes shining like suns we greet each other in circle.
The portals are forever there, offering resistance to invite our push.
Gather in – and the future can unfold.
We stand on generations, all woven into nature.
Will you step where you were meant to be, where you can be seen, so the world can go on, more full, with you so clear?

—Sandra Capellaro

WEEK 5

SENSATION AND REFLECTION

The trail emerges as you sniff it.
—Susan Harper

CENTERING

Begin to settle yourself, wherever you are. Allow yourself to drop any effort it took you to get here. Notice the quality of how your body is meeting the ground and how it meets you.

Attend to the sensations of breathing. Perhaps you sense a coolness at the tip of your nose as you breathe in; the touch of air as it moves along the inner surfaces of your nose and the lining of your throat; the inner sense of expansion in your chest; a stillness at the end of the inhalation; a shift, subtle or dramatic, as inhalation turns into exhalation. See if you can stay present to a complete cycle of breathing sensations.

As you continue to settle, go into lunar breathing in which you attend, on the exhalation, to the sensations in the back of the throat. Offer each breath as a caress, savoring the experience as you would with someone you love. Notice what is occurring through the landscape of your body and, without the need to name the sensations, how one follows another.

Photo: **KATHY CASSENS. SANDRA CAPELLARO** *in* "*Venus*", *choreography by* **ELAINE COLANDREA**

Then bring your hands to your chest and offer the sound of M there. Again, let each breath-sound be offered with care, seeking out the direct experience of the sensation of the movement of the sound. Repeat the M sound, slowly, two more times, following the sound and sensation with your attention.

Move your hands to another location on your body for another slow series of three slow M breaths. Repeat again, moving your hands to a third location.

Pause to notice any after effects of the breath, sound, and touch.

THE NATURE OF SENSATION

Sensation is the primary language of the body. If you consider sensation to be a language, movement practice is a way of learning this language. This involves listening, interpreting, responding, and engaging in a kind of dialogue. The wordless communication of your organism is felt as subtle variations of sensation, which, as you notice them, become more and more precise and eloquent while remaining simple and direct.

Sensation is continuous and changing; this is its essential nature. It is important to understand that *sensation is actually movement.* Like a fluid, sensation is continuous and changeable, and it is taking place in every aspect of the body as a whole. There are so many thousands of simultaneous tiny movements, electrochemical exchanges, and intercellular communications going on every second, that no one knows how much of this is possible to feel in a conscious way. Movement practice provides the opportunity to explore these seemingly infinite realms of sensation. By willingness to experience the subtle sensations just beyond your usual range, you expand your awareness of the choices available to you for how to respond to any given situation.

Sensation comes to you as direct experience, something you feel viscerally, a primary way of knowing. To experience something directly is qualitatively different than learning from a book or from another person. What you learn through sensation is never really forgotten, although it may not be known at the conscious level. It reaches beyond what can be encapsulated in words. It originates in the silent experience from which all meaning arises and has its own value. It is a way of feeling your aliveness. Its function is not to "get" you anything; rather, its value comes from connecting you to your genuine life force.

Finding your way through life is a challenge. When you develop the capacity to relate to and trust the movement of sensation, it can serve as a touchstone and guide. The changing landscape of sensation is something you carry within you and is always available for you to access as a source of living information.

ENGAGING WITH SENSATION

The process of engaging with sensation can be described as an inner dialogue between "you" and the sensations that arise one after another as you move. An essential aspect of this movement practice is to cultivate the art of engaging with sensation and becoming more experienced, skilled, and creative in doing so.

Each person is a living organism with an innate capacity to learn, adapt, and innovate in response to new sensory information.

At some point in movement practice, you are likely to encounter sensations that bring up associations or memories, whether of particular feeling states or potent events in your life. There are many ways to work with this kind of material, depending on its content and intensity as well as on your intentions, interests, preferences, and level of experience. For instance, you could go into a practice session aware of feeling tension or a "negative" emotion, and intentionally invite the sensations to come forward so you can attend to them, follow their lead, and notice associations that arise.

There is a moment, before you conclude that a sensation is pleasurable or painful, good or bad, before the sensation reminds you of some feeling or event, in which it is just a sensation, a sensation in relation to which you can remain open and curious. You remain with it in an attitude of inquiry. In this moment you can inquire: What is this sensation? What are its qualities? How does it move and change? It is the literal, felt movement of sensation that teaches you.

Pause. Rather than quickly backing off and labeling the feeling as "bad," you may simply pause. The listening pause—the moment of refraining from action—is the opening to engage a new sensation and choose whether to follow its movement into unknown territory.

You always have the choice of how to respond to sensation: move toward it, move away from it, move with it, or simply be with it. There is no wrong choice. This gives you great freedom to explore and can elicit a relative sense of safety.

Slow down. Once sensation is experienced, especially slowly and fully, in a context of safety with moment-to-moment freedom to choose—what was unknown has become known. The system reorganizes so as to encompass new information. The world of the familiar has expanded.

This sense of safety is increasingly vital to health as social institutions dissolve, nature itself is under threat, and we are called to participate more creatively in our own lives and with one another to meet the unknown. Humans need a sense of safety in order to re-imagine and move toward the world we wish to inhabit. A state of fear or chronic anxiety holds hostage the underlying flow of sensation and feeling inherent in the experience of aliveness.

As you slow down, begin to inquire into the sense of safety: What does it feel like? How do you recognize it? What part of your body is more alive when you feel safe?

Exert less effort. By exerting less effort in a given movement, a more subtle level of movement can be sensed. Movements of the small muscles, such as those used for very delicate tasks, actually produce more sensation than the exertion of large muscle groups and increase the flow of neural information.

What is important is the context of safety with freedom to choose at each point. This could mean giving yourself permission to proceed at your own pace, in your own way, and to say "enough for today—time to come to a close" when you choose. In this context, you can experience the sensation as a movement in its own right, with its own information to deliver, however it moves you.

Learn to trust the flow of feeling. As you go through the rounds of your practice, you come to understand that there is a flow of feeling which is changeable, adaptive, responsive, and occurring within the body all the time. To tap into this flow of feeling, to gradually learn to trust its continuing presence, is to access the flow of life as an embodied experience.

It is the awareness of sensation, untied to other scripts and accepted as intrinsic to the flow of life in the body, that loosens the grip of past experiences in which one had to hold oneself in a particular way in order to cope. As Jungian psychologist Michael Meade writes, "The defenses necessary to preserve the integrity of one's spirit during the early stages of life become life-threatening later on, keep one isolated from the flow of life, and poison the inner waters of the soul." (Michael Meade, *Men and the Water of Life: Initiation and the Tempering of Men*, [San Francisco: Harper, 1994], 329).

As you proceed in your practice, remember that you are working with the ongoing flow of sensation, allowing it to inform you, surprise you, and bear you to a state of greater well-being.

REFLECTION

This week we invite you to reflect on the language you use to describe your movement experience. Reflection as we are using the word is more than thinking about your movement experience. It is about capturing, in words and/or in pictures on paper, some part of your experience.

By naming sensations, you are cultivating the language of the body, widening the lens of acceptable sensation, and enriching your movement repertoire. Here are some suggestions:
- Use textural "feeling" words rather than going into an emotional, rational, or anatomical interpretation.
- Seek neutral language, especially for "negative" sensations.
- Describe sensation in terms of something you remember feeling in the past, a physical memory.
- Borrow language from other activities familiar to you—like cooking, gardening, observing animals, being in nature, or anything in your daily experience.
- Remember that what you put to paper need not be lengthy, elaborate, neat, or complete. Rather, let it be another form of engagement with movement and sensation.

PRACTICE SEQUENCE: EYE-WORK

- Review breaths and sounds from previous weeks
- O Sound
- E Sound
- Theta Breath
- Lunar Breath
- Reflect on sensation

Much of the quality of your attention is held in the eyes, particularly in way the eyes are constantly fixed in the same position. Most of the time, the focus is forward, directed towards an object, screen, or destination. Interesting things may start to happen on a sensory level if you can let go of the forward focus. Here we invite you to simply pay attention to your own experience for a few moments, with a more structured piece to follow. Moving the eyes in a gentle way can help "unfreeze" a pattern of holding in the tissues of the body.

It is important to go gently with yourself in this practice and know that it is not intended to erase all previous holding patterns in one practice session. Part of the value of a personal movement practice is that it allows you to truly slow down to the rate at which your own system is ready to open and feel. Every practice session is in itself another layer and expands your ability to experience aliveness and freedom, as well as a full range of emotion.

1. *Baseline/open attention.*

Begin by closing your eyes softly. Feel how you are, sitting comfortably or lying down. Notice the character and texture of your breathing. Become aware of any dominant sensations and how gravity is moving through you.

Let a word or phrase come to you to describe what you are experience. For specificity, you might attend to a particular place in your body. How dense or spacious is the feeling there? What is the texture of sensation? Is there a sense of movement? Write or draw to represent this in a tangible form, while staying connected to the flow of your practice.

2. *Moving the eyes.*

Consider the fluid nature of your eyes. With your eyes still closed, let your attention center on one of your eyes. Begin to allow that eye to move in a gentle, patternless way, without pushing or forcing. It might be a whisper of a movement, letting the fluid-filled orb of the eyeball move. Then relax the eye, letting it go and fall back to its center.

Repeat this two to three more times with the same eye, gently moving the eye in an unusual path and then letting it go and falling back to center.

3. *Return to baseline.*

Come back into open attention, letting go of all effort. Notice any new sensations arising, or perhaps differences between the two eyes or a shift in the area of your system you noted before.

Again, let a word or phrase come to you to describe what you are experiencing. Write or draw to represent this in a tangible form while staying connected to the flow of your practice.

4. *Repeat steps one through three with the other eye.*

5. *Introduce breath and sound.*

Begin another layer with the eye movements by introducing one of the sounds you have done before (the O sound, the E sound, the theta breath, or the lunar breath). Repeat steps one through four, allowing the movement of the sound to blend with the movement of the eye. Notice the change of sensation with the addition of a sound-breath vibration. Repeat the sound three to four times, slowly and attentively. Then drop back into open attention.

6. *Movement exploration.*

As you have shifted the holding patterns of your eyes, notice where movement may be newly arising in your body. Feel free to go into movement exploration as it calls to you.

7. *Closing baseline/open attention.*

PRACTICE AND JOURNALING

Assignment 1: Practice at least two times this week (more is great).
- Practice allowing enough time to layer the sequence two or three times.
- If your time is limited, just do one round of this week's sequence. Or, do the basic practice (lunar breath, M sound and lateral drifting) for five to ten minutes, two times this week.
- After each practice session, make notes. What did you do? What sequence did you follow and where did it lead you? What kind of sensations did you notice?

Assignment 2: Synthesize your reflections.
- Review the notes and/or images you made during and after each practice session. What feelings, sensations, and/or insights did you experience while doing this? Write about the process of including reflection as an active, tangible part of your practice.
- How can reflection deepen your experience of embodiment throughout your day?

DRENCHED IN THE LAKE OF AWARENESS

Pausing in the early morning candlelight
Before sliding behind the mask of a life:
A covering to obscure
The real bare wildness of daylight—
Of heartbreak and fear;
A mask of obligations, promises and regrets
So thick that breath cannot find itself—
Is almost imperceptible.

On days like this
Hope is unfounded,
Faith is veiled,
Love is buried.

Yet there is a fragrance of a memory
That finds itself through my skin, my feet,
my sinuous stretching:
The direct experience of a vibrant life in the lake of awareness.

A unitive exuberance returns
Across landscapes and times,
Emulating an essentially human aliveness
That brings things unfounded,
Veiled and buried,
Rushing into the morning—
To be touched and felt again
As the return of hope,

A river of faith,
A cavernous love—
Breaking through the barriers of habit,
Winding their way into a moment of grace.

In the darkest days
The presence of great love
Cradles and comes again.
Comes as the simplicity of beauty found
in each shifting of light and color,
The illumination of mystery—
Moment by moment,
Breath by breath,
Life by life.

—Beth Pettengill Riley

WORKING WITH PAIN

Pain is one of the most challenging human experiences. What choices do you have in how to approach pain? How can you work with pain? What actually *is* pain?

Your inner monologue might be something like—Oh, there's that pain. I've had this pain before. This pain lasts a long time. I don't think I can do what I was going to do today because of this pain.

To begin with, you could drop the word *pain*. This alone opens up a path to creative innovation around the place of difficulty in your body.

In the context of your personal practice, there is an opportunity to open a dialogue with the sensation. You inquire, what is this feeling? What are the dimensions of the sensation? Is it thicker in the middle and thinner and more porous around the edges? Does it move? Perhaps you notice movement within the area of intense sensation. How does your breath move in that area?

Stay focused on your breathing. You might feel the breath touch the edges, diminishing the intensity there or even increasing it in a more localized way. If the area feels immobile, like concrete, move your attention slightly outward to where the movement of breathing can be felt, yet still close to the

GALE MARSLAND, *Conjuntio Oppositorium*

place of immobility. These are ways of touching pain with your attention and gaining information.

To move toward an intimate experience with what you do not prefer is the invitation that sensation offers. You can ask, how did I notice this feeling in the first place? What are words that accurately describe what you feel—without the loaded word *pain*? Could you describe your experience as a texture or a movement? Thick, dense, dark. Perhaps an image comes to mind or a memory, which when named creates another kind of movement capable of refreshing your relationship to the original experience.

When you say, and especially when you write, these words, you reframe the sensation of pain, refine your experience of sensation, exercise your imaginal capacity, draw on your sensory memory, and give value to this language of the body. You begin to hone in on the texture of this particular experience in your own body. The words you use to describe your experience open the door to a wider range of possibilities. In this way, working with pain can be a powerful motivator for practice and an initiation into becoming the author of your own experience.

Long-time Continuum and Buddhist practitioner, Darlene Cohen, suffered from debilitating rheumatoid arthritis. She practiced in order to touch the moments between the pain and then lived out her days with a wisdom that can only come from profound personal and direct experience:

> If we practice paying attention to our body mainly to get rid of our suffering or restore an ailing body to functioning rather than to express our life and our nature, it is a very narrow achievement. Just as the clay Buddha cannot go through the water or a wood Buddha cannot go through fire, a goal-oriented healing practice cannot permeate deeply enough. We must penetrate our anguish and pain so thoroughly that illness and health lose their distinction, allowing us to just live our lives…Healing ourselves is like living our lives. It is not a preparation for anything else, nor a journey to another situation called wellness. It is its own self; it has its own value. (Darlene Cohen, *Finding a Joyful Life in the Heart of Pain*, [Boston: Shambhala Publications, 2000]).

GRACE

How is it that grace happens?

When I have suffered long
lost hope of any comfort
dropped the battle out of weariness

Fall to stillness
Fall to darkness

The unknown draped over me

From a deeper depth it rises
From a distant star it comes

Softly touches my cheek
whispers in my ear
traces my lips
opens my eyes
and gazes at me

—Raine Brown

WEEK 6

A MOVEMENT PRACTICE TO SUSTAIN YOU

CENTERING

What sustains you? For now, let the question just float. Become present to where you are now.

The gravitational field of the earth is moving through your bones. Breath is rising within your core. Let yourself settle, aware equally of your surroundings and your inner state. Notice your belly relaxing, the skin of your face untensing, your eyes settling in the hollows of your skull. Notice the movement of air as it enters your nose and the subsequent subtle cascade of movement and sensation touching the inner surfaces of your body.

Carefully and without force, follow your inhalation and exhalation. Perhaps you sense expansion in the ribs, perhaps a subtle undulation of the diaphragm as it moves, perhaps a pause at the end of the exhalation. Gradually, everything settles, as if your skin were simply resting on your bones.

NIKI BERG, *Dreams and Fantasies: Orange*

Settle, open, loosen. Take a series of three or more slow lunar breaths, sensing the exhalation coming through the back of your throat and spreading through your whole body, steadying and enlivening.

Now take one simple O sound, the sound traveling through the fluid in your spine, from tailbone to head, like a minnow swimming upward along the cerebral-spinal river.

Then pause, and gradually shift your awareness back to the space around you.

SUSTAINING YOUR PRACTICE

How are you, how is anyone, to keep a practice going? The universe offers you an open invitation to begin and to continue to practice. Your acceptance of that invitation expresses a commitment to your own life process and to the larger ongoing-ness of life. *How* to sustain practice is an individual challenge for each person. We can get distracted with life, imagining that other things are more important, and we can push away the desire to live an embodied life. Nevertheless, the invitation remains, sometimes feeling like a demand, a faint whisper, or a desperate call, and sometimes feeling like a warm welcome from a reliable companion.

Consider reframing the question, "How do I sustain a practice?" to instead ask, "What sustains me?" Reflect on the idea that people show up for the things that sustain their lives, financially, physically, emotionally, intellectually, socially, spiritually—and above all, personally. When something rises to a certain vital level of importance, people clock-in to work on time, get to yoga class, take their medication, visit relatives, show up at a protest march, and so on. That which could be voluntary or discretionary is felt as necessary. Somehow, you know it is not optional, even if you don't exactly "feel like doing it," and even if you don't see anyone else around you doing it.

LIVING AS A FLUID BODY

Water is the primary sustenance of all life on earth. Moving fluidly becomes a primary value when you recognize that it is vital to your life force, the full expression of living well that you long for, and that there are few other activities that meet this need. When you experience your practice enlivened as an expression of life force, it sustains you and becomes something you *want* to do.

In this final week we offer you an inquiry into what it means to live as a fluid body, in a fluid world, as a fluid process. Our intention is to offer inspiration for you to maintain contact with yourself at a primary fluid level and assist you in sustaining your practice. The shift of perception—understanding that the essential nature of the body is fluid and identifying yourself as a fluid process—is part of the momentum that may sustain you. Once that shift is made, it becomes possible for your practice to become not only a private experience, but also a larger reverberation that has meaning and relevance in building the "more beautiful world our hearts know is possible." (Charles Eisenstein, *The More Beautiful World Our Hearts Know Is Possible*, [Berkeley: North Atlantic, 2013]). In this way your practice can become the foundation of action in the world.

The full scope of living fluidly means that no matter how frozen, how numb, how stuck you feel, *movement*—the movement of breathing, the movement of fluid—is always there, if only as the smallest signs of life. The fluid movement within you, intrinsic to the life of the natural world, exists and moves according to forces and principles larger than you, which can lead you to new resources and to understanding what sustains you.

To undertake personal practice as an inquiry into the essence and possibilities of movement is to revive yourself, remember your fluid origins, reconnect to the ancient river that flows through all life, and relearn its lessons. It is to open yourself with intention and awareness to participation in the profoundly fluid nature of existence and to accept this into your personal experience of life.

WAVE MOTION

Water is the primary sustenance of all life on earth, including the human body. Living fluidly, you feel nourished. When you feel nourished, a full scope of wholeness is realized in your health, work, and relationships, allowing you to be of service to the world with complete presence.

Wave motion is the expression of water in the movement of the body. The wave motion of breath is the primary source of fluidity in the body. Breath moves in cycles that rise, peak, and subside. Experiencing your body as a multiplicity of fluid densities whose motions affect one another begins to show you why water is so essential to life. Water is not only a substance that fills and surrounds our cells; the way water moves is the way our tissues first moved. The patterns of fluid movement, down to the most subtle and technical details, are found within every aspect of human physiology. This is neither by accident nor without consequence, as every kind of fluid movement supports the structure and function of the organism as a whole.

In this sense, wave motion, the movement most often associated with water, is the body's primary medicine. The movement of water, carrying the primary message of life through the body, is translated to awareness through the language of sensation. When the body has become bound by cultural conditions—stress, illness, fear, or trauma—wave motion offers nourishment and restoration.

Although wave motion may be brought about as something you "do" by initiating subtle movements, these movements also arise spontaneously, entwined in the process of breathing or felt in the wake of movement in which you have just engaged. At its essence, wave motion is present at all times in tissue which is not being "held still." When you make any sound, including the breaths and sounds used in the practice we have outlined in this book, vibrations penetrate your tissues, which then begin to vibrate in response, setting the stage for wave motion.

Understanding the body as fundamentally fluid, wave motion "feeds" it. The wave motions of the natural world are never repetitive, and—like ocean waves, breathing, and heartbeats—every wave cycle is different. In the body, heart rate varies subtly even over each breath cycle, speeding up slightly on inhalation, slowing slightly on exhalation. Breathing itself changes from moment to moment. Variations arise spontaneously to restore homeostasis, adapt to present needs, and bring in fresh information. When cut off from the natural world, entrained to repetitive mechanical sounds and surrounded by the high frequency vibrations of electronics, the body craves the nourishment of wave motion.

PRACTICE SEQUENCE: WAVE MOTION

The practice we offer this week invites you to become like water. To become like any substance, object, or creature—or like something you saw in a dream—is a human capacity that invokes the power of the imaginal realm to bring forward knowledge, wisdom, and healing for one's own benefit or for the common good. Another way of describing this is the ability to merge your consciousness with something else.

To access the intelligence of fluid, you first have to move like fluid. Simply moving as if you were water has the power to drop you almost instantly into a fluid experience of yourself. You will feel for yourself how this changes your relationship to the space and things around you. It is from this shift in awareness that we invite you to form your question and further your inquiry. How can movement practice be the foundation of action in the world?

1. *Baseline visualization.*

Start sitting or lying down. Notice your breathing and its quality, the weight of your body and the sense of its density, and the presence of internal movement, if any. Follow several complete breath cycles before you move on.

Bring to mind a stream in nature, where water is flowing. It could be a creek or a river that you have known in your life. Now it flows near you. In the moving water you notice different currents—streams within the stream—forming arcs and spirals, ripples and swirls, gushing and splashing, whirlpools and waterfalls.

Now, slowly dip your hand into the water. The water passes between your fingers, touching the skin, lifting your fingers. The water is a pleasant temperature—refreshing.

Notice the quality and shape, and the way the water moves you and invites you to move.

Gently dip your wrist into the stream and let the wrist, hand, and fingers move with the currents. You notice that you can press back into those currents, reshaping them slightly. As your hand moves, the water's path changes. There is an interplay as the water's movements shape you, and your movements reshape the water. You lift your hand through the water in different ways, following the currents with your fingers, letting your hand play with the water.

Your arm becomes immersed up to the elbow. The whole forearm is now moving with the water.

Now you gently immerse your whole arm, including the shoulder. Feeling the currents move around your upper arm, you may sense subtle movements within your arm and extending into your neck and head.

Continue to explore for several more minutes, keeping to the side of the body you started with. Stay true to your sense of the stream, its myriad currents, the ways the water moves you, and the possible awakening of currents within you. As you allow, the sense of immersion and response extends down into to your torso on the same side, and further into the hip and leg.

Let the waters around you recede. Pause in open attention, breathing and taking note of the experience of stillness. Notice the difference between the two sides of your body. One side might feel lighter, less dense, with a sense of internal movement.

Repeat the water immersion visualization on the other side.

2. *Take the movement of water into your spine.*

Move onto all-fours. Starting at the tailbone, begin a series of "O" sounds moving up the spine. Let the O sound and the movement of water that you have just invoked weave together, reaching into the fluid core of your spine. As you continue to sound, with pauses between each breath, allow the awareness, sound, and movement to travel up the spine, through the neck, and into the cranium until your whole spine is moving fluidly.

3. *Experiment with other places in your body.*

As you have done with the spine, bring the O sound and the movement of water into another place in your body, perhaps a place that has not been not moving freely. Proceed slowly, invoking the movement of water in and around that area, and notice what occurs—what quality of movement arises.

4. *Return to baseline/open attention.*

Gently, bring your exploration to a close.

As you come to a close, again pause in open attention—taking in the sensations in your body, gradually giving language to what you have experienced, and making notes.

The reward of a fluid movement practice may come down to a sense of freedom that resonates through one's whole being. The movement of water as experienced in the body is at once profoundly familiar and yet imbued with a sense of discovery, new possibilities, new dimensions of experience, and an entirely new way of being.

PRACTICE AND JOURNALING

Assignment 1: Keep practicing! Practice this sequence at least once this week. Invoke the movement of water as you have done in this session. You may experiment with layering, change of position, and different breaths.

If your time is limited, do just a part of this week's sequence, or return to the basic practice (lunar breath, M sound, lateral drifting) for five to ten minutes, at least two times during the week. Take notes at the end of each practice session.

Assignment 2: Review the following supports to practice that you have already encountered in this course:

Rely on the movement of water. Water is the true teacher. Remember that the movement of water is with you always, as a guide. Water is moving within you every moment, and as you practice you will find it easier (and more "normal") to invoke the sense of water—not only in your practice, but also in everyday life and in difficult moments where tension is mounting or you think you cannot handle it. You can always rely on the movement of water.

Rely on the space and time you have created for movement practice. You may need to experiment with ways of taking time for practice until you find what works for you. Regular engagement is an important aspect of practice, a form of layering, a means to make something new become more familiar, and a moment to compare doing the same thing on a subsequent day or explore the potentialities within the limits of your space. Your "space" can be a physical space or a space in your schedule, or both.

Rely on and review the basic elements of a moving inquiry: the movement of attention, the movement of breath, the movement of sound, the movement of movement, the movement of sensation.

Draw from, explore, and gradually expand your palette of movement, sounding, and breath. You could start at the beginning of the course with the simple practice and go through each week again. A beautiful aspect of this work is that even if you "repeat" a particular sequence, you are different each time, and as you bring your attention to the newness of the experience, it will yield something unique.

Rely on the methods and principles of layering, broadening your dynamic range through variations in breath/sound and changing your orientation to gravity.

Remain open to the unexpected, which may lead you into movement exploration. Opening to movement variation, slowing down, suspending, pausing—any of these may launch you in an unexpected direction with the possibility of discovery. Through this kind of practice, you become ready to receive the unexpected insight, the genius of your own body who appears, saying, "Thank you for inviting me. Here's what you need to do now in the realm of movement."

Rely on sensation as a portal to a life that has depth and meaning for you. Use your senses throughout your day as a means to remain tuned in to the natural world. Underneath the movement of human culture—something that *seems* so real—there is the reality of the earth, the air, the sky, the horizon. There is the movement of life, the movement of the cosmos. Continue to uncover the "why" of movement by gazing beyond the veil of culture to a larger wholeness, to what feeds your soul and brings you into the field of belonging and nourishment, which some would say is akin to the nature of love.

FURTHER WAYS TO CONTINUE GROWING YOUR PRACTICE:

Keep learning through classes, workshops and retreats. Finding a teacher offering Continuum classes in your region or signing up for an extended workshop or retreat can be one of the most important things you do to sustain and deepen your movement practice.

The reasons for this are many. Throughout human history, across all cultures, people have come together for ceremony, celebration, and sustenance, usually including sound (music, chanting, singing) and movement (dance, ceremonial movement). Communal experience is vital to individual health and wellbeing, and something like it occurs (though usually not explicitly) in temporary communities created in ongoing movement classes, workshops, and retreats. Getting out of your day-to-day routine—whether for a day, a weekend, or longer, especially in a natural environment—is likely to shift your perspective, and the shared immersive experience can have lasting healthful effects. You will always learn something new.

Have fun with your practice. Just have fun! Bring something to the practice that interests you and that you look forward to. As they say, make it your own. Some people like to use card decks, such as a tarot deck or inspirational cards; you pull a card and use it to create an intention for your practice that day. You may find inspiration and organic structure in other ways: the seasons, the elements (earth, air, fire, water), wisdom texts such as the *I Ching*, and other sources. Working with specific props (a ball, foam roller, stretch fabric), or with distinctive music and sound (tuning forks, bells, singing bowls, and so forth), can further your inquiry.

Consider the concept of the "gong." The term *gong* in Chinese Taoist tradition implies a personal commitment to follow a particular practice (such as meditation) for a specified number of days. It can be especially useful in developing a genuine relationship with any practice so that it becomes a part of your life. To simply commit to forty-five days of thirty minutes of daily practice can be quite doable, whereas an open-ended intention to practice two hours per week for the rest of your life can remain always out of reach.

THE JOY OF PERSONAL PRACTICE

No one can tell you where your practice will lead. Sometimes your practice will just flow. At other times, it requires more effort. And at certain times of your life, you may wish that your practice would bring moments of delight, yet you find them so elusive that eventually you realize it is time to give up on the wishing. Then, may your longing ripen to curiosity, rather than turn bitter with a too-soon dismissal of the whole idea. Yet moments of delight and surprise arrive on their own. When they do, you know they are "real," beyond what you wished for or could have planned.

We hold to the truth that there is an intelligence in the body that always leads to health, insight, and wholeness. The book you hold in your hands is dedicated to that conviction.

TRAVELER XXIX

    Walker, the path is your footprints,
    And nothing else.
    Walker, there is no path,
    The path is made by your walking.
    As you walk you establish the path,
    And when you look back
    All you see is the trail you left
     On which you will never set foot again.
    Walker, there is no path,
     Only white-crested trails in the sea.

                    —Antonio Machado, translated from
                          the Spanish by Marcella Bottero

DESIGNING YOUR OWN SEQUENCE

Our intent with this section is to establish you more securely in the confidence of practicing on your own. Creating your own sequences is a step toward making your movement practice "real" and relevant to your life. In an important sense, *your felt sense of aliveness is the center of your life*. Your practice, like everything else in your life, relates back to that elusive center.

Movement practice places you in a process through time, larger than yourself. At the juncture of the personal and the universal lies the progress of one's own life, the undeniable draw and propulsion to explore, discover, overcome obstacles, broaden one's scope, and move toward wholeness. In this regard, to create your own movement sequences is an answer to a fundamental need for innovation expressed by all living systems. Fully felt movement offers a way to attend to, embody, and follow the call within yourself, even if—especially if—it is not articulated in words.

At the same time, the ongoing-ness of practice connects you to a community of others who engage in this kind of movement practice. What many wisdom traditions describe as the most basic aspect of health is the flow of energy through the body, and also through one's life. It is a continuous, ongoing flow that keeps one constantly refreshed and healthy. Around the world, there are many practitioners of fluid movement, so at any given time, day or night, when you engage in your own practice session, know that there are others who are doing so, too.

How do you put together a sequence of your own? What is there to guide you? In the language of Week 4, *the sequence is the container*, so another way of posing the question is to ask, how do you create a container for yourself?

At the outset there are a few things to remember.

Most movement traditions, like yoga and the martial arts, have come to modern people as systems of preset poses and movements, making them relatively straightforward to translate into

KAREN LYKKE GROTH, *Untitled*

home practice. By contrast, in the kind of practice we are outlining here, neither the movements nor the sequences are fixed.

So, following a sequence of your own design will always feel different than stepping into a container set up by someone else. When you create the sequence for your personal practice session, there is no escape from meeting yourself. There is no one to push you out of your habits. And to practice on your own feels different than in a group.

Perhaps the first guideline is to notice whether you are making value judgments. For most people, judgments are pretty common in the stream of consciousness. For some, in the absence of an outside teacher the analytical mind goes into overdrive. We invite you to summon the practice of self-referencing here—to simply be with your own experience and not compare it to others or judge it as not good enough. There are no "bad" choices in the sounds, breaths, or movements you choose, and there is no good or bad way of feeling sensation. It is just how you happen to do it now. You are cultivating a new skill. Rather than—*Do I like this sensation? Is it good for me?*—you are learning to ask, *What is this sensation?* and *How shall I respond?* This allows new information to come forward. As you stay open to new experiences, unexpected directions, sensations, thoughts, and feelings can arise. As Continuum teacher Susan Harper has said, "The trail emerges as you sniff it." Developing a personal practice is not just about how you move along an established trail, but about discovering a new trail each time you move and continuing to sense it as you go.

CREATING A SEQUENCE

1. *Be guided by your own situation at this time.* Follow your curiosity and passion as you create a sequence and then use this sequence over a few days or weeks, until the need has been met or another need arises that is drawing your attention.

What do I need now? Let this be the originating question for your practice time. If you have not been practicing weekly, this might be an important ingredient for you, because one of the keys to personal practice is *to find your own way in*. Sometimes it is enough to lie down on the floor and the need presents itself through sensation: a longing to breathe freely; a desire for relief from acute pain; a recognition of emotional distress; an urge to dance, to feel your strength, or get upside down; a longing for rest—these are just examples.

Part of what makes practice "personal" is the ability to tune it to your felt needs. Even as you repeat a sequence over time, inevitably you will sense changes, whether in yourself, the movements, their effects, or what they signify.

2. *Decide how long you intend your session to last.* Set a timer to free yourself from having to check the clock. Turn off your electronic devices and put them in another room.

3. *Keep it simple.* Select no more than two or three components to work with for your first self-designed exploration. These could be drawn from those we have offered here or others in your experience. You probably need more than one, but the point is to keep it simple. This conscious selection forms an entry point

into a flow of sensation, which once begun may become a fresh source of new information, ideas, and guidance.

4. *Repeat your sequence.* Ideally, repeat your sequence three times within a given session. Change your relationship to gravity in the second and third rounds. That is, if you begin the first round lying down, you could begin the second sitting or on all-fours and in the third round return to lying down. Use whatever variation of orientation to gravity that calls you.

5. *Allow for unplanned movement exploration.* Allow yourself the opportunity to move "beyond the container" as described in Week 4. You may notice spontaneous movement arising more easily as you continue to work with the sequence.

6. *Pause between each layer.* Take a full pause—dropping all effort, simply receiving—between each round of your sequence. Go into open attention. This time is truly "open."

7. *Write notes after your practice.* Describe or list what you did, sensations you experienced, and any insights that came to you. Drawing and poetry are also possible ways to express what comes forth during and after practice.

8. *Listen to your own living system.* It is easy to fall into the trap of trying to follow what you think a personal movement practice should look and feel like. Instead, consider: *What does it take, all by yourself, to actually listen to your own living system?* "What it takes" resides in the willingness to become an insider to your experience, rather than an outside observer or judge. It might mean giving yourself a long practice session (say, one to three hours) once in a while, so that you can give over your attention, fully and lovingly, to your state of being. With that sense of tender curiosity comes the possibility of a fresh awakening or an unexpected result. In the end, practice may be less about what you *do* than the quality of the attention you bring to it.

Finally, it may be useful to remember that people use practices of all kinds to change habits, to learn new skills, and to expand their minds. By cultivating a different kind and quality of movement you uncover a different way of being. Although getting started may take effort, regular practice acquires a certain momentum of its own, because the result of practicing is meeting a fundamental need. When you notice that something is "off" because you have not had your practice time, this is the moment you begin to feel the power of practice.

LOVE

May you touch every place,
you love every being
as the first time and forever.
May you live the first time,
forever.
May you love with no reason.
No track of you.
Love without somebody.
May you always be yourself
the One and Only
in Love.

—Claudia Catani

ESSENTIAL READING

The books on this short list are among those we consider most important in developing a sense of the fluidity, intelligence, and aliveness within nature—and hence, within one's physical being.

Schwenke, T. *Sensitive Chaos: The Creation of Flowing Forms in Water and Air.* East Sussex, UK: Rudolf Steiner Press/Sofia Books, 1965.

Jenny, H. *Cymatics: A Study of Wave Phenomena and Vibration: Volumes 1 and 2.* Newmarket, NH: MACROmedia Publishing, 2001, (vol. 1 originally published in 1967, vol. 2 in 1974).

Buhner, S. H. *The Secret Teachings of Plants: The Intelligence of the Heart in the Direct Perception of Nature.* Rochester, VT: Bear & Company, 2004.

Conrad, E. *Life on Land: The Story of Continuum.* Berkeley: North Atlantic Books, 2007.

Gintis, B. *Engaging the Movement of Life.* Berkeley: North Atlantic Books, 2007.

Little, T. *Yoga of the Subtle Body: A Guide to the Physical and Energetic Anatomy of Yoga.* Boulder, CO: Shambhala Publications, 2016.

Ostakeski, F. *The Five Invitations: Discovering What Death Can Teach Us About Living Fully.* New York: Flatiron Books, 2017.

Poetry, like movement practice, is rooted in the human inquiry into *being* and has the ability to shift experience out of the trance of everyday life. As companions to practice, we recommend also the works of writers such as (for starters) Rumi, Kabir, Hafiz, Rainer Maria Rilke, Mary Oliver, David Whyte, Mark Nepo, and Lisel Mueller.

ACKNOWLEDGMENTS

The authors wish to thank Elaine Colandrea and Watermark Arts for helping in countless ways to bring this book to life and for supporting the original online course, which took place in 2017. At that time, the need for a guide to Continuum was evident, and Elaine entered our partnership bringing an adeptness at collaborative creation as well as providing an online home for the project. Later, with the transcripts from the online version and Elaine's ongoing encouragement, we dove headfirst into creating this practical guide to embodiment through the lens of Continuum.

Watermark Arts is based on a foundation of personal, generous, and reciprocal relationships. The vibrant artwork and eloquent poems in these pages come from Watermark's online galleries, featuring the works of artists and poets who are themselves Continuum practitioners. For permission to use these works, which make the book much more than it would have been otherwise, we offer thanks to Mary Abrams, Noelle Adamo, Niki Berg, Raine Brown, Sandra Capellaro, Claudia Catani, Suzanne Wright Crain, Bobbie Ellis, Prue Jeffries, Karin Lykke Groth, Satya Kirsch, Gale Marsland, and Dennis Matthies (for permission to use works by Barbara Mindell).

SUZANNE WRIGHT CRAIN, *detail from Sa Nou Pa We 2.0; Noted by the artist: This cloth holds the energy of a call to action. The name is derived from the tradition of Voudou and means "that which is hidden but always there."*

In addition, we thank Maryanne Gallagher for the detailed awareness she has brought to this project as our dedicated reader and keen-eyed friend. Maryanne was a member of the original participant group in the online course and has steadied the course of the book as we morphed and grew the words and concepts into this whole offering. Her heart and spirit are in the pages themselves.

We thank Emilie Conrad for her vision, genius, and creativity in allowing the work of Continuum to unfold without regimentation or reduction in scope and meaning. The decades-long partnership of Emilie and Susan Harper allowed the work to gain traction and unfold a depth of humanness that we, to this day, find difficult to manifest through any other modality. Susan was instrumental in this aspect of Continuum in particular and in innovating the flexibility of shapings of the work that continue to unfold.

Finally, we wish to thank all of the Continuum teachers and practitioners who have stayed the course since Emilie's passing in 2014. Because of them, in the last five years many people have been drawn to the depth and transformative nature of the work. It is with gratitude that we honor each and every person who feels called to engage in this work in their own lives and with others. In so doing, they tend to our collective human birthright of living well in our bodies in this tenuous and fragile time.

AN ARTS MOVEMENT INSPIRED BY SOMATIC AWARENESS
WATERMARK ARTS

Photo: **KATHY CASSENS. E. ELISABETH PETERS, GISELA STROMEYER, SANDRA CAPELLARO** *in "Venus", choreography by* **ELAINE COLANDREA**

ABOUT WATERMARK ARTS

Watermark Arts brings together somatic awareness and artistic expression
in the belief that both are essential aspects in creating a more humane and peaceful world.
The word *soma*, from the Greek *somatikos*, implies a fullness of presence
in the living, sensate, wholeness of bodily being. With awareness of the integrity of the body,
comes a felt experience of the interconnection of all living things as part of a larger whole.

In our modern, technologically-advanced era, somatic explorers exist near the cultural edge,
holding this way of wholeness in the face of a widespread and pervasive sense of fragmentation.

Artists, too, live at the edge of culture, working with revolutionary ideas
and symbolic messages encoded in dance, poetry, stories, music and visual art.
As culture creators throughout history, artists have brought about substantive, peaceful change in society.

These times call on us to become generators of the culture we wish to live in.
Creative acts show up in all aspects of life — in art, in teaching, in community-building.
Watermarks asks, What happens when these creative acts are informed by somatic awareness?
Can we bring into being a world permeated by a sense of wholeness and interconnection?

WWW.WATERMARKARTS.COM

ABOUT THE AUTHORS

BETH PETTENGILL RILEY is a global leader in somatic movement education and therapy, as well as a seasoned somatic movement activist with over 40 years of experience in facilitating workshops in Continuum, yoga and meditation. She has a master's in education with a specialization in dance from Stanford University and currently serves as president of the board of the International Somatic Movement and Therapy Association (ISMETA). Beth passionately engages embodiment as a spiritual path and maintains a private practice in Santa Cruz, CA, assisting individuals in finding greater freedom of movement.

PRISCILLA AUCHINCLOSS has been seeking to understand how the world works for most of her life. She earned a doctorate in experimental physics from Columbia University and, as a professor and administrator at the University of Rochester, investigated the role of gender in the culture of science. Finding in movement a way to reclaim a more authentic, elemental and physical life, she left the university, opened a movement studio, and became an authorized teacher of Continuum. She lives and works in Rochester, NY, and continues to explore movement as a path of insight into the world and healing the modern soul.

View from Priscilla's home office, 2016

www.ingramcontent.com/pod-product-compliance
Lightning Source LLC
Chambersburg PA
CBHW041422300426
44114CB00005B/90